MONEY SELF-TALK

TALK YOURSELF INTO A LIFE OF WEALTH, PROSPERITY, AND JOY

KRISTEN HELMSTETTER

*Green
Butterfly
Press*

ABOUT THE AUTHOR

In 2018, Kristen Helmstetter sold everything to travel the world with her husband and daughter. She currently splits her time between the United States and a medieval hilltop town in Umbria, Italy.

She writes romance novels under the pen name Brisa Starr.

Listen to *Coffee Self-Talk with Kristen Helmstetter* wherever you listen to podcasts.

You can also find her on Instagram:

instagram.com/coffeeselftalk

OTHER BOOKS BY KRISTEN HELMSTETTER

Coffee Self-Talk: 5 Minutes a Day to Start Living Your Magical Life

Lipstick Self-Talk: A Radical Little Self-Love Book

The Coffee Self-Talk Daily Readers (#1 & #2): Bite-Sized Nuggets of Magic to Add to Your Morning Routine

Pillow Self-Talk: 5 Minutes Before Bed to Start Living the Life of Your Dreams

Wine Self-Talk: 15 Minutes to Relax & Tap Into Your Inner Genius

Tea Time Self-Talk: A Little Afternoon Bliss for Living Your Magical Life

The Coffee Self-Talk Guided Journal: Writing Prompts & Inspiration for Living Your Magical Life

The Coffee Self-Talk Starter Pages: A Quick Daily Workbook to Jumpstart Your Coffee Self-Talk

Coffee Self-Talk for Dudes: 5 Minutes a Day to Start Living Your Legendary Life

Coffee Self-Talk for Teen Girls: 5 Minutes a Day for Confidence, Achievement & Lifelong Happiness

DISCLAIMER

I am not a financial advisor. I'm also not a voodoo mama with a crystal ball. I am a woman who is on a crazy adventure with money, using a cool self-improvement tool called self-talk. I'm simply sharing *my* story here. Results are not guaranteed, and your results may vary.

NO SPECIFIC OUTCOME OR PROFIT IS GUARANTEED.

*This book is dedicated to my mom, who always used to tell me,
"Throw enough shit at the wall, and something will stick."*

She was right.

CONTENTS

INTRODUCTION

Dear Reader,

Five years ago, my family was housesitting in France, caring for two dogs and six cats. The house was located on several acres of wooded land that I walked every day, taking in the silence and the beautiful, red autumn leaves falling around me. But during this time in my life, I had overwhelming anxiety about our finances...

We were buried under $100,000 of debt.

On one of those days, as I walked up and down the long driveway of the country house, my feet crunched over the white gravel, and my heart raced uncomfortably. There I was, walking through this idyllic French countryside, and I should have seen nothing but beauty. But instead, all I experienced was crushing anxiety.

I mean, autumn leaves don't pay the bills.

It was time to figure something out.

So with my cuticles stress-bitten and bleeding, I took a shaky breath and started to create a plan for how we could pay off the debt.

And I did what I'd always done... I shifted into crazy overplanning mode.

I thought about the income we had from different sources between my husband and myself, and I scrutinized our expenses. I crunched numbers to figure out how many products we'd have to sell, plus how many hours of consulting my husband would need to bill, in order to pay off the debt in a year or two.

Basically, I came up with a practical solution to our debt problem. And even though the plan was daunting, it was not insurmountable. In my mind, I simply structured a way to go from A to B to C ... all the way to Z, paying off the debt.

That's how you do things, right? By the numbers?

It made sense at the time. So I took a deep breath of the French country air, and I assumed my typical attack mentality because, you see, I was a *can-do* type of woman. A Type-A personality who worked like a machine. I approached tasks and projects like a robot, and I got the job done. You wanted something handled? I was your gal!

So that was my plan: Tackle the debt!

But there was something I didn't realize. All this time, my life was being slowly strangled, completely controlled by two vicious demons: *fear and scarcity*. And they were stealthy bastards, living in the shadows, hidden from conscious view. They went unnoticed, disguised as normal traits like discipline, prudence, and the habit of making spreadsheets. You know, all that Type-A stuff.

And as I went about executing my A-to-Z plan, life moved slowly, and the needle on our debt moved even slower. I was still anxious. Nails and cuticles still bitten. And panic started taking center stage. Sometime later, I learned how detrimental these dual emotions of fear and scarcity were, and I realized I had to change. This realization eventually led me to create my life-changing Coffee Self-Talk routine, in which I started each day by turning off social media and email during my morning coffee, and instead, I read positive affirmations filled with words of gratitude and self-love.

My new self-talk changed how I looked at money. Instead of fear, I started to create new opportunities for myself. Instead of thinking that money would make me happy, I flipped the script:

If I could make myself happy first, the money would follow.

And that's exactly what happened.

The results of completely changing my mindset speak for themselves: A little over a year later, I was completely out of debt. A year after that, I had half a million dollars in the bank.

Through the process, I discovered that going from A-to-Z to pay off my debt and create a prosperous life *wasn't the only way* forward. I realized that maybe I didn't need to be *so* practical and uptight with my strategy. After all, life is wiggly, full of curveballs—so I got bendy with it! And I'm glad I did, because I live completely differently now when it comes to money, and it feels miraculous.

And that's what this book is about: Changing your mental approach to building wealth and prosperity.

This isn't a traditional book about investing, budgeting, financial equations, or cutting coupons. Those books already exist. This book is different... it's about *preparing your mind* for receiving wealth.

Why?

Because this is an important part of the process of creating wealth, prosperity, and joy. It's much harder to receive them until your mind and heart *are ready* to receive them.

This book teaches you how to do that.

Here's the thing... I've always appreciated money and prosperity. But for most of my life, I didn't possess what I call the *Magical Money Mindset*. Or an intimate *relationship* with money.

But I do now. And in this book, I'm going to share it with you. I'm going to teach you, step by step, how to have the same kind of relationship with money that flipped my life from living in fear to living in abundance.

Using my *Money Self-Talk*, I reprogrammed my thinking about money. I changed my attitudes about spending and saving. I took bold actions that directly turned my finances around. Best of all, I dove into new dimensions I never knew existed. Places where fear and scarcity were no longer cracking the whip on my butt.

In short, I changed not only my mindset, but my *energy* when it came to reaching my financial goals. And I created a brand-new relationship with money. I took on a sparkly new attitude that attracted everything I wanted. It felt like magic, but it's not... it's neuroscience. My new thinking caused me to have new beliefs and take different actions. Actions that took my life to a whole new level.

I transformed my relationship with money into a *partnership*. Money was no longer my master, or a quest... *it was my ally*. With this transformation, an extraordinary shift of financial possibilities rushed through me, and I started on a great new life adventure.

We all know money doesn't buy happiness. But here's the thing... it gives you a heck of a lot more freedom. And choices. *And fun*. It won't solve all your problems, but it will instantly solve A LOT of them, such that you can free up the mental resources to focus on the other stuff. Driving on bald tires? Buy new ones... problem solved. Need a new roof? Buy one... done. Your child is struggling in school? Hire a great tutor... done.

As for the non-financial problems—maybe you've got health issues, or a difficult relationship, or you're at a crossroads in your career—I want you to consider two things:

First, financial resources can often be a super useful tool in helping you solve many non-financial problems. For instance, money won't make you lean and healthy, but it sure does make it easier to eat healthy and join a gym or buy a Peloton.

Second, and more important, when you free yourself from the fear and scarcity mindset, something amazing happens... *your true self flourishes.* You become more relaxed. Your anxiety melts away. You're more patient with loved ones. You do better work. You get better sleep. You're able to comfortably take risks that have the potential to catapult your life to new levels.

All of these come from rewiring your brain, which is the direct result of changing your self-talk.

I can't make promises about what will happen to your bank account, or how soon. But what I can do is teach you the process that reprogrammed my brain and built the Magical Money Mindset I used to build up *my* bank account.

I'll warn you now: It's a *bold* mindset. Brash, even. Hell, I publicly proclaimed to the world in a blog post that *"I'm going to become a millionaire"*... when I was over a hundred thousand dollars in debt!

But it's not just about talking big, or "fake it till you make it." No, it's a shift in mindset that harkens back to your starry-eyed youth, when anything was possible, when play and imagination reigned. It's a mindset that says, *There's an easier **and more fun** way to do this.*

But we also don't discard the practical. Plans filled with practical steps for becoming wealthy have a place in this program, but these plans get supercharged by the magical vibe that comes with adopting the Magical Money Mindset.

Creating a different life means doing things differently. It means showing up and doing the work, but maybe not "work" in the way you think. It means doing the steps to reprogram your brain, thus changing your beliefs, thoughts, and feelings. It means making different choices and being intentional with your day.

For all of these, filling your mind with powerful Money Self-Talk is the first step on your exciting new adventure.

When I changed my money mindset and began my money adventure, I felt this strange sense of destiny, like everything would somehow be okay—*even though I had no idea how*. I just knew I was ready to turn up the fire on my finances, because I was ready to go BIG. And boy, was it big!

I want to help inspire you to embark on *your own money adventure*, in which you get to choose who you *want to be*... with respect to finances, money, abundance, wealth, and prosperity. Where you get to rediscover and redefine yourself.

You have the right to reinvent yourself, and your life, today.

Before we begin, you must know something: *You are amazing*. Even if you don't realize it yet. You have insane wealth right between your ears, right now. Inside your skull, there are stories and experiences. And opportunities! I know, because I have these, too. And you can use that to make money. But it takes confidence... and belief... and a powerful money mindset.

And just know that if something seems weird or uncomfortable as you create your new Magical Money Mindset, *keep at it*. If necessary, read this book again, and again, so you can feel its power welling up inside you, as you imagine everything you want to achieve. Fire up the confidence and take action to bring your new financial destiny to you. Remember... it only works if you do the steps.

And don't worry, I'm here with you every step. Let's do this together!

Wishing you wealth, prosperity, and joy!

Kristen

THE GOAL OF THIS BOOK

The goal of this book is to help you bring more abundance into your life and to help reduce stress and anxiety about money. This process happens by *changing your mindset* about money and about yourself. And this is primarily done through your "self-talk." (More about self-talk in Chapter 1.)

Money Self-Talk is divided into 26 chapters, and each chapter includes a Money Self-Talk *script*. Each self-talk script has affirmations about prosperity, joy, and well-being. These affirmations are the thrust of this book, and you'll want to read these scripts regularly to reprogram your brain for building wealth, prosperity, and joy. When you're done reading this book, you'll continue using the Money Self-Talk scripts regularly going forward.

Feel free to read the book at your own pace, but you'll want to read one of the scripts found at the end of each chapter once a day, if possible.

My Routine

Personally, when I'm working on manifesting financial goals, I read my Money Self-Talk script(s) every morning for my *Coffee Self-Talk*. If you're familiar with Coffee Self-Talk, then you know what I mean. However, if you're new to my work, then let me briefly share a bit about the life-changing ritual that is Coffee Self-Talk. It's a special morning ritual with a specific task: reading, thinking—or ideally, speaking out loud—scripts filled with specific words designed to rewire your brain, change your thoughts, your beliefs, your behavior, and your life. It also immediately makes you feel amazing, empowered, and happy.

The Coffee Self-Talk ritual basically involves taking five minutes every morning, while I'm drinking my coffee, and reading my self-talk affirmations. During this special time, I'm not messing around on social media or diving into email first thing. No. I start my mornings with the most powerful impact by priming my mind for living my best life: That's my Coffee Self-Talk. Now, Coffee Self-Talk time can be used for self-talk of any kind (general wellness, health, career, relationships, magical living, etc.), and of course, it can be used for money and abundance. Hence, this book.

So while you might read through the book only once, you'll return to it regularly to read the provided Money Self-Talk scripts. (Or you'll read scripts that you write yourself. More on that later.)

CHAPTER 1

WHAT IS MONEY SELF-TALK?

What you're thinking is what you're becoming.

— MUHAMMAD ALI

Self-talk is the words you say to yourself and the thoughts that run through your mind every day, from the moment you wake up to the moment you fall asleep. It's how you react to what people say and do, whether it's the news you're watching, or Instagram, or the outfit your coworker is wearing. It's your thoughts, beliefs, opinions, judgments, praises, and criticisms you say and think about everything... other people, the world, and in particular, *you.*

When you have a thought, it's your self-talk. It's how you see life. Some people see life as scary, whereas others see it filled with possibilities. Some people feel financially broke and focus on that, while others stay open to opportunities and possibilities for abundance, no matter how much money is in their bank account.

The important thing to know is that your self-talk directs your emotions and your focus, and these, in turn, direct your actions and behaviors, which determine almost everything about your life.

If you've ever wanted to know *THE secret* to improving your life, or reducing stress, or achieving your goals, or loving yourself more, or being happier, or getting in shape, or having better relationships... *or changing your finances*... the answer is always the same: It comes down to your self-talk.

> Change your self-talk, and you change your brain.
> Change your brain, and you change your behavior.
> Change your behavior, *and you change your life*.

Everybody has self-talk. But most people do not take conscious control of their self-talk. The easiest way to do that is by reading written scripts of positive self-talk, every day, until it sinks in, becomes your habit, and you've retrained your brain to think and talk in a way that's consistent with the kind of life you want to create.

Here are some examples of generic positive self-talk:

Today is a great day. I like feeling good.

I love me just the way I am, today.

I choose to feel good about myself, because I'm worthy.

I achieve because I persevere.

I'm tapping into good feelings right now. That's the key to success.

This is fun, and I'm ready for my day.

As you repeat affirmations like these to yourself day after day, your brain begins to internalize them, and act on them, to make your actions consistent with the words.

Your brain will do this whether the words are true yet or not. It will also do this whether you believe them or not. But the really cool part is that, in a few weeks (sometimes even sooner), you will actually start to believe the words. And in very little time, they become an accurate description of the new, happier you.

The self-talk affirmations you say each day can be about anything you'd like to focus on: general well-being, health, fitness, career, relationships, spirituality... anything you want. And it's a good idea to address different aspects of your life at the same time.

In this book, we're going to focus on the themes of:

- Prosperity
- Abundance
- Wealth
- Success
- And of course... *money!*

When you're doing self-talk about these things, we call it *Money Self-Talk.*

Money Self-Talk

Money self-talk is what you say and think about all things financial, such as your income, spending, saving, investing, prosperity, and abundance.

Perhaps even more important, your Money Self-Talk is also what you say that *indirectly* affects these things, such as your *beliefs* about your own abilities, self-worth, and how the world works financially. For instance, whether you generally believe it's hard to eke out a living and save for retirement, or it's fairly easy to become financially secure, or even mega-wealthy. And everything in between.

Do you think it's easy to make money? Hard? Do you think the world is out to get you, or that opportunities are everywhere? Do you believe you're lucky? Unlucky? These are all examples of your Money Self-Talk.

Everybody has self-talk... it's how our brain works. We think things, almost constantly. Self-talk can be either positive and helpful, or negative and harmful. And we all have thoughts and beliefs about money. For most of us, the things we tell ourselves about money are mostly unconscious. Just part of our inner dialog that's always running in our heads.

But these words are important. They're *powerful*. They dictate what we do, and what kind of lives we live. They ultimately determine whether we live lives of scarcity or abundance. Whether we're rich or poor.

Here's the good news...

You can take control of your Money Self-Talk!

You can make it do whatever you want. Instead of letting this process run mindlessly in the background, you can specify *exactly* what you say to yourself. Initially, you do this through conscious effort, through repetition as you read the Money Self-Talk scripts provided in this book, or that you write yourself. But soon, this new way of talking and thinking starts to become your habit, such that your new positive self-talk takes over and replaces the old, negative self-talk that may have been holding you back your entire life.

By taking control of your Money Self-Talk, you're taking control of how you interact with money. You deliberately create for yourself a mindset and vibe of abundance, and you use positive affirmations in a radical way to attract prosperity to you, and to inspire your actions.

And sometimes, the results seem a bit magical, like the time I had linked to a product on my blog and forgotten about it, and then one day, I received a $700 affiliate check out of the blue. While unex- pected windfalls may seem magical when they happen, they're usually the result of our past behavior and numerous things clicking together, some of them within our control, and some not. Okay, maybe with a little sprinkling of pixie dust! :)

The big picture: It's really simple... think great thoughts about acquiring money, and you start to see more ways to acquire money.

And the more you believe, the more you become more willing to take the necessary actions.

But if you think poor thoughts about money—like debt, scarcity, and lack, and stay focused in that poor mindset—and those guide your actions instead, it becomes much harder to reach your financial dreams.

Again, your brain doesn't care if what you tell it is true or false. It acts on the instructions either way. It doesn't care whether you choose happy, "rich" words, or crappy, "poor" words. Your brain's interest is in proving you're right, whatever your thoughts are.

And this gives you *incredible* power, because the words you use are *your choice*—no matter what. It's always *you* who chooses which instructions you give to your brain. And you can increase your confidence with positive self-talk. You can sky-rocket your self-esteem to beautiful new heights with positive self-talk. *You can radically change your prosperity with self-talk.*

But above all, it changes how you *feel about yourself.*

Money Self-Talk makes it possible to truly love yourself and feel worthy of prosperity—no matter what you've been through. And self-love is critical. If you don't love yourself, it doesn't matter how hard you work, or what strategies you attempt—you won't feel worthy of succeeding. And if you don't feel worthy, your subconscious will follow your lead on that... and it can wreck your otherwise perfectly good desires.

If you're new to self-talk, you might feel strange saying the words at first, or even silly! That's totally normal. Some people even cry the first few times, because they realize they've lived their whole lives without feeling worthy. Without loving themselves. And some people feel weird and skeptical about the whole thing. If any of these describe you, no problem, just stick with it. In no time, these words and thoughts and feelings will feel like second nature.

They'll feel intrinsic, like they're part of your soul. And at some point in the future, it'll be hard to imagine your life without them.

> *Positive thinking and positive attitude attract prosperity, peace, and happiness.*
>
> — ANURAG PRAKASH RAY

Writing Your Own Money Self-Talk

Although I provide you with numerous Money Self-Talk scripts in this book, I recommend that you write some of your own as well. Only you can come up with the words that focus on the most relevant points for your situation and spark the happiest emotions inside you. You are the one who knows you best, and only you know what language lights up your brain and fuels the fire in your soul.

1. Write in First Person

Always write, speak, and think your self-talk in first person. First person is necessary for making "you" both the giver and receiver of the programs that will rewire your brain. It's the easiest way to get straight into your own head and heart, helping you feel the words faster.

For example:

I am relaxed and feel peace.

I love my life.

Money always finds me.

I am wildly rich.

I am crazy-cakes successful.

2. Write in the Present Tense

Writing in the present tense creates a sense that the result has already happened, or that it's happening right now. Not tomorrow, not next month, not next year. Do this even if the thing you want hasn't happened yet.

For example:

I am supremely wealthy.

My products and ideas are loved by millions.

I make a lot of money, and I make a difference in the world.

I have tons of creative ideas for businesses.

My investments are growing at all times.

Remember, you're doing this to reprogram your brain. You want your brain to start acting *as though the thing you want has already become your reality.* You can make your dreams real by thinking about them in the present tense. If you want a life of total freedom with your schedule, then you want to feel free *right now.* If you want abundance and wealth and prosperity, then you infuse yourself with feelings of that *right now.* The language you choose helps you do that.

Speaking as though the future has already happened may feel strange at first, but it will soon feel natural, and this technique is very effective for training your brain to "act as if." As the saying goes, *fake it till you make it.*

In essence, you're teaching yourself a new way of speaking, very similar to practicing a new language. To train your brain correctly, you must speak the way you want to think after the training has happened. If instead, you were to speak in the future tense, with aspirations such as, "I will become financially independent," this state will always feel like it remains in the future, from your brain's point of view, and it will not change your actions to make it happen now.

3. Use Elevated Words

Use words in your Money Self-Talk scripts that spark elevated emotions and uplifted feelings. Choose awesome words and thoughts that make you feel really, *really* good. You want words that make you feel amazing, with emotions such as:

- Awe
- Gratitude
- Generosity
- Love
- Excitement
- Power
- Creativity
- Relaxation
- Happiness
- Joy

The trick to accelerating your results is to *feel the feelings you'd have if you were living your dream life today*. Neuroscientist Dr. Joe Dispenza says that the greater emotion and feeling you tap into, the greater your vibe gets broadcast into the world, and the faster your goals become reality. He says,

> *The greater your energy, the shorter the amount of time it takes*
> *for your manifestation to appear in your life.*

4. General vs. Specific Affirmations

When you write your self-talk scripts (or modify the scripts provided in this book), you can get very specific and detailed, such as specifying the exact amount you want in your bank account, or how many rooms or square feet there are in your dream house. The amount of money you want in your paycheck, or how many trips you take each year.

Your goal is to create specific, vivid pictures in your mind. Why? Because clear pictures will cause stronger emotions to sparkle inside you, which amplifies the entire process of reprogramming your brain, upgrading your strategies and actions, and busting ass every day toward your goals.

That said, not all lines in your script must be specific. A mix of general and specific is ideal. You should also include broad statements like, *I am wealthy. I am rich and generous.* These also pack a prosperous punch.

5. Inspiration from Others

Add any awesome affirmations you find elsewhere, or favorite passages from books, song lyrics, quotes, or other words that inspire or uplift you.

6. Repetition

In the Money Self-Talk scripts I provide in this book, you'll often see lines and themes repeated. This is intentional, as repetition helps program them into your brain faster and more strongly. If you write your own script, choose an important line to say more than once. I recommend that, if you write a 20-line script, choose one or two lines that are most juicy to you, and repeat them three times throughout the script. That said, you could even have an entire script with the same two or three lines repeating the whole time. It's impossible to have too much repetition with self-talk. The more times you say a positive affirmation, the better.

My Primary Money Self-Talk Script

Below, I share part of the main Money Self-Talk script that I use personally. I often use this for my morning Coffee Self-Talk time, and I also do it in the middle of the day by listening to a version of it I recorded on my phone's memo app. (For extra emotional impact, I recorded it with inspiring background music, something I discuss in the book, *Coffee Self-Talk*.)

As of this writing, not all of the affirmations in my personal script have come true yet, but I think and say them with conviction, *as if they were true*. So be warned, my money scripts are filled with bold words, and I use very strong affirmations.

Kristen's Personal Money Self-Talk Script

I continually experience overflow with money and riches, because wealth, prosperity, and joy shine all around me.

I love money. I trust money. Money supports my beautiful, playful self.

All of my finances are always up, and up, and up. All the time. Attracting bigger, earning bigger, donating bigger, saving bigger.

My money loves to replenish itself in my bank account. It wants to.

I have anything available whenever I want. I can always manifest more. This is who I am.

Money is a consistent, reliable part of my life.

I elevate myself and live with an incredible mindset about abundance, prosperity, and money. I keep going. I keep growing. I keep moving.

I am a brave, calm, and wealthy woman who trusts myself. I am safe to spend, invest, release, and attract money. I know that more and more is always coming to me. I'm ready.

I am here to tap into my own shimmer-shining soul. I listen to my own fun and creative truth. I create what I feel destined and called to create.

I pay attention to what pulls and dances inside my soul.

I'm open to the magic that's all around me.

It is safe to follow my truth. My heart is safe.

My creations are meaningful and changing the world.

I have opportunities all around, all the time.

I'm living the jet-set life. I show up. I am the master conductor of my life. I do it. I am doing it!

I just have fun, and the money comes! I'm on a blazing, new, awesome adventure with money!

I get to create a beautiful life of my design. I'm the master conductor. I am love, I am success, I am in the right place, at the right time, doing the right thing. Always.

I am more than enough, and every aspect of my life is easy-breezy fun. Abundance is all around me.

Relaxation is a key to manifestation. Easy does it... flow, flow, flow. Relax. It's a balance between intent and surrender, and it feels so amazing to have money come to me so easily. I have opportunities all around me. I am creative and having fun.

Money is fun. Money provides easy solutions and answers. Money works for me all the time.

Money is circulating around me all the time.

My work changes lives, and I'm making the world a happier place, one person at a time.

I'm so grateful. I'm overflowing with gratitude.

I enjoy creating, and I have an abundance of time to create, play, love, and do whatever I want.

Money expands my soul. Money amplifies me.

Money exists to support me. I am abundance.

I. Am. Worthy.

So there you go! Fun, huh? As you can see, I've incorporated all kinds of affirmations for what having money means to me personally.

The scripts provided in this book are about fifteen lines each, but as you can see from my personal script above, scripts can be any length you want. Sometimes my Money Self-Talk consists just one line, repeated over and over, like a mantra. Either way, try to spend five to ten minutes a day reading your script, whether it's fifty lines or one.

Reading the Money Self-Talk Scripts

Here are some tips for when you're actually doing your Money Self-Talk.

Read Them Out Loud

If possible, read the self-talk script out loud. In the beginning, if you're not comfortable reading your script out loud, that's okay. But trust me, it gets easier once you've done it a few times. And it makes the process more fun and has a stronger impact. Not only are you reading the lines with your eyes, but your ears are hearing it. Your mouth is feeling the words. It's more sensory. You can even whisper the words if you want, as that creates its own special magic. Sometimes I whisper my affirmations into my mug of coffee, like I'm a good witch casting spells over my brew. And therefore, over my life.

Or go wacky and wild! Some people dance while saying (or singing) their affirmations out loud, with music playing in the background. Your *movement energy* provides tremendous power.

Personally, I change it up all the time. Sometimes I stand. Sometimes I sit. Sometimes I sing. All that said, it's perfectly fine to read quietly, but I find it to be more powerful when I say the words out loud.

Feel the Words

With self-talk, one of the most important things is to make sure you resonate with the statements. So while I provide powerful Money Self-Talk scripts with the chapters in this book, if you don't resonate with my language, then definitely feel free to change anything you like. Or perhaps you like the language I use, but you need to use details specific to your situation. No problem, just add lines that make the most sense for you.

Read It Twice (or More)

When you do your Money Self-Talk, I highly recommend you read your chosen script a couple of times in a row. (Or read it repeatedly for the duration of time it takes you to drink a cup of coffee in the morning.) So, whether you decide to stick to the scripts in this book or you write your own... and whether it's fifty lines, ten lines, or one line, give yourself a good five to ten minutes with your Money Self-Talk each day. The more you show up to your life and use powerful self-talk, the faster the changes will happen.

That's Money Self-Talk in a nutshell. Read a script of positive money affirmations daily, multiple times a day, weekly, or whatever you like. Say it, sing it, dance it, shout it, laugh it. Heck, translate it into another language you're learning, and say them both!

But whatever you do, *show up*. You have to show up if you want it to work. You have to actually *do your self-talk* for it to change your life.

Okay! Here you go, your first script of the book. Use the instructions above as you take your time to read through it twice. Feel the words, create pictures in your mind, and believe.

Money Self-Talk Script

I choose my self-talk, and my self-talk designs my life.

At all times, I am in charge of what I say and think, and I choose magnificent words and thoughts.

I love feeling rich, and I know that prosperity is all around me. Yeah, baby!

It doesn't matter what's going on outside, I choose what's going on inside, and this helps change my outside!

I am worthy of my desires. We all are. And I am grateful.

I am kind, generous, and rich with feeling. Yesssss!

What I seek also seeks me. Thank you.

I am ready to reinvent my honeyed-moneyed self. I have desires deep in my soul, and I'm opening my arms for everything I want to come to me.

I am comfortable earning tons and tons of money.

I love the power I feel in my veins to design the illuminating life I want. The power of feeling vivacious now, no matter what, and I hold the master key to the kingdom of anything I desire.

I shed my old identity, and I'm walking through my new life, always fresh, always bright. I'm ready for it all. I love the ride of my life.

I shape my life by starting with my mind. I am powerful like this.

I claim abundance, prosperity, gratitude, and joy.

I am inspired to live my greatest life. I am worth it.

I am peaceful and happy, and this brings more peace and happiness into my life.

Exercises

How is your self-talk today? Is it generally positive, generally negative, or somewhere in between?

What words about abundance resonate with you and spark the most joy and power within you?

Are you willing to commit to doing your Money Self-Talk every day? If so, commit to it now.

CHAPTER 2

PRACTICAL VS. MAGICAL

I dream my painting, and then I paint my dream.

— Van Gogh

This book is different than most finance books. I approach abundance and success from a mental point of view, and specifically, what I call the *practical* and the *magical*.

For example, when it comes to increasing my own income, I might consider taking practical steps, such as sitting down to write a book, taking classes to improve my skills, doing research online, placing advertisements, doing interviews, and launching social media campaigns.

But I also take advantage of a *magical mindset*.

My energy plays a huge role in making my success either extra hard or extra easy. Just to be clear... I prefer *extra easy*! You see, it is possible to be successful with only a straightforward, practical approach. But like I said, it's easier or harder based on your *energy*.

And what is "energy"?

Energy, as we're using the word here, is about your *vibe*. Your feelings and emotions. It's the extra oomph that makes you leap out of bed, excited to tackle your to-do list. It's what makes you feel great while you're taking all the practical steps toward building wealth. It infuses a kind of happy glow in everything you do. It also causes you to do better work, create more value, work better with other people, and see more possibilities.

This is the magical stuff I love. Am I putting out a happy vibe or a sad vibe? When I feel happy, I stand taller, I smile more, and I attract and see more opportunities. I have more energy to go after my goals, and my self-worth is boosted. But if my energy turns frumpy and grumpy, then my efforts feel weighted down, like I'm slogging through quicksand.

The magical includes all your emotions. Let's take gratitude, for example. The more gratitude you have, the more you realize you have to be grateful for, in a feedback loop. I live by the mindset that "what I appreciate, appreciates," and that includes love, health, and of course... money. Simply by thinking about money in these terms—as something to be grateful for—you automatically create a mindset that sees money as a positive thing in general. Not something to be feared, or to be controlled by. In this way, by focusing your energy, you take control of what money *means to you.*

The funny thing is that none of this is mystical or *woowoo*. It's just how the brain works. The more you smile, the more opportunities you draw into your life. When you're in a good mood, you're *much* more likely to be successful, at whatever you're doing. Take advantage of this all the way to the bank!

Some people call this magical aspect of success the "Law of Attraction." And maybe it is. I think there's a lot out there we don't know, and I admit, some very strange synchronicities have happened in my life that have boosted my success. More often than not, things just line up for me, like dominos. Sometimes in freakishly strange ways that seem to defy reason. I don't always have an explanation for it.

Was it the result of my own subconscious actions? Dumb luck? Quantum juju pixie dust? Who knows. But I'll tell you something... it sure *feels* magical.

Regardless of the mechanics of how manifestation, uh, *manifests*... I'm convinced of one thing: My success is 100% due to my powerful mindset.

I'm also not the first person to use mindset and energy to change their finances. Successful people have been doing it from time immemorial. I've simply put my own spin on it... such as creating fun, outlandish affirmations that amplify my efforts and results. I'll be sharing these with you throughout this book in the Money Self-Talk scripts.

Here's the thing... If you *want* something new, it usually means *doing* something new. It means looking at things with new eyes. With wonder and awe. With... *"what if?"* questions whirring around in your soul. It means acknowledging both the practical *and* the magical.

Sarah Blakely (the billionaire founder of Spanx) talks about the "Universe" and "receiving signs" in her process. She recently wrote on Instagram:

> *Today marks a huge milestone for Spanx and for me personally. People have asked for 20 years, "When will you sell Spanx?" And for 20 years, I would say... I'll just know. Well that day is today... Start. Jump. The world needs you. Never underestimate what you could do if you truly cared the most. It wasn't what I knew (zero background in business), it wasn't who I knew (no one in the industry). I received a sign from the universe 21 years ago to start the company, and I received another sign that it was the right time to take in a partner.*

Signs. Intuition. Feelings. The "Universe." They're all part of "the magical" that I talk about throughout this book and when I discuss using self-talk to raise your energy and make new connections.

Of course, there are technical aspects as well. The *practical* stuff. Sarah Blakely didn't just sit on her ass and have a box with a billion dollars appear out of thin air. She *made* that billion dollars appear. How? She *took action*.

The Key to Success

The bottom line is that approaching your financial goals using both a practical and magical mindset is the key. And the truth is, the practical and magical *have always been interwoven*... but not everybody sees it this way. With all the practical books and information out there about personal finance, budgeting, investing, etc., the part about managing your emotions is something of a best-kept secret.

Years ago, I took an online drawing class with my daughter. I knew nothing about sketching, or drawing, or painting. I was a woman in her late thirties still drawing stick-figures. Seriously.

But I was interested in learning, because my husband and daughter are great artists. This was when we were preparing to travel the world, and I had visions of us traveling across Europe with sketch-pads in our backpacks. I imagined us sitting in front of the stunning Trevi Fountain in Rome, with all three of us sketching it. But to make it a better experience for me, I'd need to learn more about drawing, hence, the art class.

When thinking about the practical and magical aspects of living, I'm reminded of this class. During one of the lessons, the teacher taught that, instead of drawing the actual item you see in front of you, you were to *draw the space* you saw that bumped up to the border of the item. In other words, imagine a naked tree in the winter, with all its leaves dead and crunchy on the ground. When you look at the tree, you normally see the bare branches. But instead of looking at the naked branches, you're now to see *the space* between the branches. That's what you draw: the space.

Mind blown! I'd never thought of drawing the space around the item instead of the actual item. It felt downright magical, and I discovered you can draw a whole outline of something while never having really drawn the item itself. The space is unseen, yet it was always there, guiding my pencil if I acknowledged it. And vice versa... you can draw the item, the tree's branches, the practical stuff. You can't have one without the other, the space or the object... they're always both there. It's just that with the magical "space," most people don't see it. But when I started looking at things like this in my world—seeing both—it shifted my perspective and how I saw life.

ZOOM OUT: Why is it important to embrace the practical *and* the magical? Because when you embrace both, you tap into all of your amazing mental and emotional resources, making everything feel easier and more natural, like it's inevitable. Making and saving money feels more epic this way. And more fun.

I don't believe I would've had the exact same success by only chugging away like a robot doing only the practical stuff, step after direct step. I mean, maybe I would've, but I'm sure it would have taken longer, and probably been more stressful. All work and no play makes Jack a dull boy, right?

And more importantly, maybe I *wouldn't* have been as successful without the magical, because my self-talk fuels my confidence and conviction. It gives me the magical mindset and energy to make excellent choices and show up with a higher self-esteem. Both of these are priceless keys to your prosperity formula.

A man cannot directly choose his circumstances, but he can choose his thoughts, and so indirectly, yet surely, shape his circumstances.

— James Allen

Money Self-Talk Script

I build my riches using both the practical and the magical. It's an incredible way to prosper!

I am destined for wealth. I am an incredible person.

I am both lucky and skilled when it comes to making money. I have it all.

I am defined by the dream life I hold in my mind. I'm becoming someone new, rich, and full of love.

When I wake up every morning, my eyes open to all the magical possibilities around me.

I walk through my day noticing new things all the time. I am a new person.

I am open-minded, because this helps my creativity and problem-solving for more prosperity.

My riches start with my self-talk, and I believe in the power of my mind. It's magical. It's practical. It's everything wonderful.

I am grateful and bubbling with excitement for my new life. Watch me go!

I am the energy I want to attract.

I naturally attract greatness because I feel greatness.

I accept and allow myself to expand my mind more than ever before.

I know that when I keep my mind high and bright, it glows with intention, and I see the way to riches.

I am inspired beyond belief. I am motivated to move my feet. Life is amazing!

Making money is easy for me. 'Nuff said.

Exercise

Consider your life 15 years from now. Imagine that your life has progressed exactly as you wanted: You've got the career you want, success, good relationships... basically, everything you've dreamed of. Write about this future life, and explore what you'd do in this scenario. How would you spend your time? What does it feel like?

_____

_____

_____

_____

_____

_____

_____

_____

_____

_____

_____

CHAPTER 3

FEELINGS AND PROSPERITY

Wealth is the ability to fully experience life.

— HENRY DAVID THOREAU

Changing your mindset can help make your money dreams come true. But your brain isn't the only part of the formula. That's because, while the words start in your mind, they will explode with power when you involve your heart.

When you *think* good things about money, you should naturally *feel* good things about money, right? Funny thing, though... that's not always the case for some people, especially if you're overcoming a lifetime of poor self-talk. When you come from a life of financial anxiety, it's easy to doubt the idea that positive words can help change anything. It's understandable that, if you're deep in debt, it might feel insane to utter words like, *"I am rich and prosperous."* At best, you might feel very doubtful. You might even let a nasty cackle rip out of you, followed by a sarcastic *"Yeah, riiiight."*

I mean, how can words hold *that much power?*

But hear me out. The good news is that, even if you don't totally feel it yet, *you will feel it in time*. It will become your default belief and attitude. But you must repeat your Money Self-Talk scripts regularly, drilling this new way of speaking and thinking into your brain. The important thing to remember is that, the more you repeat these scripts, the more your brain will forge these thoughts into the pathways in your brain, making them permanent. Think of it like how you build stronger muscles. The more you exercise them, the stronger they become. The same thing happens with your thoughts—only it's your brain getting "stronger" with what you say and think.

The Reason It Works

As this happens, you start to *believe* it. That's one of the huge keys to this whole recipe. Because, when you start to believe what you're telling yourself, your brain starts to make it happen. It does whatever is required, and your whole life starts to change.

For many people, money is a major source of stress—filling them with feelings of lack and scarcity. It was for me too, for decades. *That is not epic living*. But when you improve your thoughts and feelings about your finances—even if you have crazy levels of debt—you'll find yourself loving life so much more. I promise.

I wrote the book you're reading—a whole book about money—not because I'm obsessed with material things, or money in general, but because I love what I *can do* with money. It gives me freedom. It gives me choices. But acquiring wealth required that I first changed how I viewed money, and *how I viewed myself*.

So one day, *I chose* to enter into a lifelong *relationship* with money. A relationship in which I saw money as *my partner*. I chose to get intimate with money. I chose to have a big, open mind about money and to keep my mindset positive about it, no matter what. I chose to be successful. I chose to believe in my destiny. *I chose. I chose. I chose.*

And you can too, because you see... *your mind is magic.* It's within the walls of your own skull that you give rise to a phenomenal mindset of confidence, abundance, creativity, wealth, prosperity, and joy. And these, in turn, push out the fear, skepticism, and doubt that are currently preventing you from realizing your financial dreams.

Money Self-Talk Script

It's my attitude that abundance is everywhere, and prosperity is mine, no matter the circumstances... because I am worthy.

I continually experience overflow with money and riches, because wealth, prosperity, and joy shine all around me.

I am grateful that I discovered the power to living a rich life, and it all starts inside my brain.

I am full of love, and awe, and generosity. These feel good, and they help make me a success.

I'm capable of great things, amazing things, incredible things! It's all happening... I feel it in my soul.

I choose to believe. I choose the words in my mind. I choose to be a success. I choose to be grateful. I choose because it's my choice!

I love visualizing my rich and beautiful life. It's fun. It's meaningful. And I'm ready for it all.

When I connect my incredible thoughts with my incredible feelings, I'm putting myself on the fast track to abundance.

I'm excited to finally be living the life of my dreams. My destiny.

I am kind and thoughtful. I am generous and loving. I am patient. All is always well.

My mind is magic, and it's full of power. My power. I am the master conductor of my life, and I choose the direction it's going.

I choose to live life as if everything I want is already mine.

I am amazing, magnificent, beautiful, strong, and full of love. I love my life so much!

I am focused and feeling my way to my prosperity.

My vibe is high, right now, as I imagine my successes, my riches, and all of the wonderful prosperity making its way to me.

Exercises

How would you describe your relationship with money? Would you consider it to be a healthy relationship? Why or why not?

What are your core beliefs about money? For instance, do you think money is good or evil? Easy to come by or difficult? What are your opinions about rich people?

Where did these beliefs come from?

Would you like to change any of these beliefs? If so, what beliefs would you replace them with?

How might changing your beliefs improve your attitude about wealth and your ability to make more money?

CHAPTER 4

THE EMOTIONAL COMPASS
TO YOUR FINANCIAL FUTURE

Success comes to those who become success-conscious.

— Napoleon Hill

Your life moves toward any given direction based on your emotions. It's like having a map, or a crystal ball. You can know something about your own future simply by observing what emotions you're feeling at any given moment. So whether it's when you wake up, or while putting gas in your car, or while cooking a steak... in any instant, you can ask yourself, *"What are my emotions right now?"* And the answer tells you the direction of your life. Are you on a road filled with potholes? Or are you driving on a road paved with gold?

I'll take the gold road, thank you very much.

I should be clear... it's not like you'll never have days without potholes. The real magic comes in how quickly you bounce back after hitting those potholes.

In Dan Harris' great book, *10% Happier*, he talks about how learning to meditate is like strengthening your "mind muscle." Most people get frustrated when they get distracted during meditation, *because they think they're not supposed to be distracted.* They see that as a failure. But the exact opposite is true... the gold lies in these distractions. Because every time you notice it happening, *and* you bring your focus back to the meditation, you strengthen your mind muscle. It's like doing a bicep curl in the gym. Each distraction-then-refocus is a meditation "rep." Without these distractions, you aren't building the mind muscle, just as your bicep won't get any stronger if you don't do any reps lifting weights.

The same idea applies here. If you experience a day with potholes and some negative emotions, don't get down on yourself. No! You need to flip that... each negative emotion is a chance to practice rebounding. Every time you flip your emotions from negative to positive, you strengthen your *prosperity muscle.* And the more you do this, the easier it gets. It doesn't matter if it takes all day to flip it, or an hour, the important thing is that you flip it. That's you taking control. That's you being the one who's *in charge of you.*

ZOOM OUT: I pay attention to my energy all day long. And I optimize it every chance I get. If I sense myself hitting a pothole of bad emotions—whether it's about the weather, finances, traffic, or relationships—I flip that shit and pave my path with gold. Like, *now.*

Flip It Tips

How do you make yourself happy when you get hit with a blast of negativity? All you have to do is think about something that makes you feel good. Anything. Right in the middle of your negative moment—you basically daydream! For example, if I feel funky, I visualize the gorgeous, second home I want... on a lake in the mountains, with tall pine trees all around. Or I daydream about love. Or coffee! Or I feel grateful for my hands and feet. Or I run Money Self-Talk affirmations through my mind, or I say them out loud. Or I send somebody else love.

I realize this is all easy for me to prescribe because I've been at this game for a long time. And that's the point: I did the work. Every time my energy tried to take a nosedive, I grabbed my sparkly lasso and wrangled that sucker back into shape. I refuse to wallow in the mud. I don't pout. I don't blame my circumstances or other people. I just fix the situation. Period.

And to fix the situation, the first step is always the same... I take control of my emotions. And with so much practice, my ability to change my vibe on a dime is incredible, which makes attaining all of my goals easier. With practice, you can do this too.

That's how you play big. That's how you shift your energy, consistently, and keep it drawing your goals to you. *Attracting* the outcome you desire. The more often you do this, the more elevated your energy will be, *ongoing*, and this will bring you more prosperity and joy.

Every notch higher in your energy is meaningful. So even if you're having a crappy day and you follow these tips, if it takes you even one notch higher... *that's great!* You don't always have to be a blazing, shooting star with the energy level of a racehorse. The point is to always level up when you can. It can be one notch at a time. Always drawing in your prosperity, inch by inch.

And if you're tempted to give this "energy stuff" the stink-eye, then humor yourself and try these techniques anyway. It doesn't cost you anything, so what have you got to lose? Besides, who's going to turn down being in a better mood?

Money Self-Talk Script

When confronted with a problem, the first thing I do is smile. And then I visualize great things. This helps me discover solutions and get back on track.

If the world throws curve balls my way, I hit them out of the park, because that's how I roll.

I'm in charge of my life, because I'm in charge of my mind.

I determine where my life is going, and it's going to the top.

I'm relaxed about my finances, and my best life is here. I am a success.

I love showing up to my life, excited about my prosperity and success. I choose positive ideas.

I'm powering up my mind every day by showing up to life. My happiness muscle gets stronger every day.

I'm vibrating on the frequency of having it all. I'm so grateful for this vibe.

I can change my vibe on a dime. It all starts with me and my words.

My life is a bright, glimmering gem because I make it so. I choose to be happy with it all, a shooting star. I'm alive... YEAAAAHHH!

I play all day with energy, joy, and sparkle, and I am capable of anything.

Peace surrounds me. Calm fills my chest. I'm rested and full of love for everything.

Money and success. Money and success. Money and success.

I'm my own gorgeous hero. I am having my moment now, the power is building in my bones. Watch me go!

Iridescent, illumination, shimmer, and shine. That's the energy I radiate.

Exercise

Make a list of things you love. You can include people, pets, nature, places, things like books, music, objects, and foods. Be very specific. Don't write "books," rather, list the books you love. Don't just write "cake," write what kind of cake. Try to fill all the lines.

CHAPTER 5

YOUR GROOVY MONEY-MAKING BRAIN

The size of your success is measured by the strength of your desire, the depth of your belief, and the extent of your persistence.

— ROBERT KIYOSAKI

When you use Money Self-Talk, it does something really cool inside your brain. It legit makes you *feeeeel really good*, because of a beautiful thing called dopamine. This vital neurotransmitter zips around your brain as a result of various things you do. We'll focus on just one of them: goal-seeking behaviors. Through a specific, goal-centered plea- sure and reward system based on dopamine, your brain works *for you* by setting you up for success.

Our brains were designed to freakin' *love* setting and reaching goals. This harkens back to our primordial days. Back in hunter-gatherer times, having goals kept us alive. In order to survive, you had to eat. And in order to eat, you had to find food. To find food, you had to go out and *look* for it. And because your brain knew you needed to look for food to survive, it rewarded you with a dopamine high every time you set out on a hunt, found a bunch of berries, or made a kill. These things made you *feeeeel* good. It made you feel motivated to keep going until you found your food, and even better when you finally got your meal.

Here's a neat little experiment. Wad up a piece of paper into a ball, and chuck it across the room into a garbage can. Do it from far enough away that it's challenging, and keep trying until you make the shot.

When you make the shot, notice how it makes you feel. There's something so satisfying about nailing the shot, especially a difficult shot. That's dopamine! Do you feel it? That's a million years of evolution at work, designed to make you enjoy lobbing stones, spears, and arrows at cute fluffy animals, during a time before McDonald's drive-throughs. But to this day, it still feels good to make the shot. In fact, we even feel it vicariously, such as the joy of watching your favorite basketball player sink the perfect three-pointer... *swish!*

That's why desire feels so good. James Clear, author of *Atomic Habits*, writes, "*Dopamine is released when you experience a pleasure, but also when you anticipate it... Desire is the engine that drives behavior.*"

See that? You get a dopamine boost even when you simply *anticipate the pleasure* of attaining your goals. How fascinating that the excitement of *just setting goals* inspires you to both *set* the goals, and *go after* them. It's an awesome feedback loop.

Why This Matters

You can take advantage of this amazing reward system in your brain when doing your Money Self-Talk. How? Because when you do your Money Self-Talk, you'll include specific goals. You'll also have affirmations that aren't specific goals, but they have the *flavor* of goals. Such as talking about things you want, things you want to become, and how you want your life to be. In other words, your Money Self-Talk *is chock full of goals*. Which means, when you read your self-talk, it *feeeeels* good, and this gets you excited about your financial goals, which motivates you to go do the things required to make your dreams a reality.

The RAS Wizard

But there's more to this incredible story in our brains! There is another system in your brain called the *reticular activating system,* or *RAS,* but I call it the *RAS Wizard* (more on this in a bit).

You see, there are millions of bits of data coming at you at all times. The impressive thing is that, at any given time, we're capable of sifting through all this data and making sense of it. In the process, we discard the vast majority of the bits, without them ever registering in our conscious minds. We have to discard these, actually. Otherwise, we'd never be able to make sense of it all. There's *waaaay* too much information. This means that, at any point in time, you're only aware of a sliver of what's going on around you.

The RAS (reticular activating system) is a precious little bundle of nerves at your brainstem, and it's fundamental to living your most prosperous life... because it filters out *unnecessary* data, so the important stuff gets through to you.

What's the important stuff? Well, it's whatever *you* deem important, based on your focus, based on your thoughts, based on your words. *Based on your self-talk.*

Are you thinking thoughts of abundance? If so, your RAS will think abundance is important, and anything that supports that view is considered "important data" to pass along to you. And that's exactly what you'll see more of in your life.

On the flip side, if you think about debt and scarcity and fear, then this RAS gatekeeper goes to work for you—just as efficiently!—to let only *that* data enter your mind.

I think of this RAS like it's the wizard behind the curtain, controlling what gets presented to me, and what doesn't. What you need to know about this RAS Wizard is that he does *not* judge what I focus on—whether it's positive or negative—he doesn't care. He doesn't decide what I should focus on—getting a different job, learning new skills, meeting new people, starting my own company, or launching a new product—because that's *up to me*. That ball is in my court—as it is in yours.

With your RAS Wizard pointing its spotlight at whatever you tell it to look for, you'll find yourself connecting to things in the outer world that match up to your self-talk. This is one of the super cool ways Money Self-Talk works: *It changes your focus to good stuff...* prosperity, money, abundance. It keeps you concentrated on the affirmations in your scripts. When you constantly fill your mind with incredible thoughts, words, and feelings, that's where your mind focuses.

Here's an example. Suppose you target your Money Self-Talk affirmations toward a dream of yours to buy a beautiful ranch in Wyoming, because you want to raise mini-moos under the big, open Wyoming sky. (Mini-moos are adorable, miniature cows.) And as part of this dream, you want a really cool, red Ford F-150 pickup truck, because you'll be doing ranch-type work, of course. Well, what happens when you start focusing on mini-moos and F-150 trucks? You just go about your normal life... and suddenly, you start to see F-150's everywhere you go!

Why? Because your RAS Wizard has new orders. Which means your brain is on the lookout for anything that might help you attain your Wyoming mini-moo goals. Now, if you also happen to see a *red* F-150 drive by with a *Wyoming* license plate (and you live in New York), then that will really get your attention! (And if it happens to be dragging a trailer full of mini-moos, well heck, that might just be a signal from the Universe to take immediate action!)

Finding Four-Leaf Clovers

I'll leave this chapter with a neat story told by Dr. Weil on the Bullet-proof Radio podcast.

On finding four-leaf clovers...

> *I met a woman once who would bet you money that from the time you said 'go' that within a minute she'd find a four-leaf clover. And she always won. And so, in thinking about this, the four-leaf clovers are always there. The problem is being able to see them... There are two aspects to seeing. There's what goes into the eye, but then there's whether the brain can recognize the pattern. And if you don't have a key in place to recognize the pattern, you can be looking right at something and not see it. So that's the case with four-leaf clovers. And I found that I was able to develop the power to find four-leaf clovers.*

Dr. Weil went on to say something else that I loved...

> *I think there's all sorts of magical stuff out there that I probably didn't see before... Things like synchronicities... If you start paying attention to them, they are there. Some people say, "Oh it's a coincidence," but that's the label on the mental waste basket that we throw certain experiences into, saying this has no significance. If you start saying that maybe this is a highly significant thing, then they begin happening more frequently, and they can guide you in a certain direction.*

Money Self-Talk Script

My brain works for me all the time by making me feel rich when I use rich self-talk.

I love setting my money goals, because it feels illuminating, sparkly, and wonderful.

All of my finances are always up, and up, and up. All the time. Attracting bigger, earning bigger, donating bigger, saving bigger, spending bigger. Up-Up-Up I go and glow. Rainbows and rocket ships! Grow-Grow-Grow.

I am ready! I am capable! I am inspired! I am ready! I am capable! I am inspired!

I see four-leaf clovers, rainbows, and pots of gold, because that's my magical focus. I decide what comes into my life, because I choose the words in my mind.

I am thankful for my phenomenal brain and the way it helps me attain my money goals.

I have anything available, when I want. I can always manifest more. This is who I am. Success, significance, and sharing.

Whatever I focus on is what I see more of in my life. It's always my choice.

I am alive with power! I am charged with glory. My life is joy, prosperity, and riches.

I have the power to create my own reality, and I choose to take action. I'm inspired!

I am grateful for the ability to choose my mindset, and I choose AMAZING!

I see the good, because I focus on the good—at all times—no matter what.

Silver linings are how I live my life. I see them everywhere I look.

I feel thankful for my incredible, freedom-filled life. I am smart. My brain is phenomenal.

I am rich, and I love to share. Everything good always comes to me. I am relaxed with everything in my life. I shine with happiness, and calm is all around.

Exercises

What inspires you to do your best? Is it a certain kind of music or a certain celebrity? Is it nature? Religion? Family? Your life philosophy?

When in your life have you been most inspired to take action or change?

What happened when you made the change?

CHAPTER 6

YOUR JOB: TO BELIEVE!

The strongest single factor in prosperity consciousness is self-esteem: believing you can do it, believing you deserve it, believing you will get it.

— Jerry Gillies

Not long ago, I was buried in over $100,000 of debt. With no prospects of paying it off. In fact, the debt was getting bigger every month.

But despite this crushing debt, I had a *rich* mindset. Most people would've said I was delusional. I believed so strongly that money was coming to me, and that all of my debt would get paid off with ease. I had no idea how it would happen. *But I believed it would.*

Belief will be one of the most important aspects of your money journey. If you don't believe in yourself, your quest to reach your financial goals will feel like walking backwards, uphill, on ice, blindfolded and handcuffed. In fact, you might never get there.

But when you believe in something... when you believe, not only in your dreams, but in *yourself*... then things feel like they just click into place inside you. There's a natural feeling that propels you, faster and faster. Instead of walking backwards up that icy hill, when you believe in yourself, you feel like you're zooming forward, like Superman.

Your Main Job: To Believe!

Your job is to *believe* in your rich future. Your job is to picture success in your brain and feel awe and excitement... no matter what your financial circumstances are today. Your job is to believe that you can have the life you want.

Because, when you do this enough times, something strange happens. You start to feel like what you want has *already happened*, even though it hasn't yet! It starts to feel normal, like it's a natural part of you. And that's because your repeated words, feelings, and attention on these "success" pictures of yourself, is how it becomes believable to your brain. It becomes real in your mind before it's actually real in the world.

This step is necessary. It's why we do Money Self-Talk. To create the belief that wealth is possible, and that we're capable of achieving it. After enough days of doing your Money Self-Talk, bit by bit, you start to *believe*.

And that's when things start to line up.

Like shiny, golden dominoes.

Visualizing Speeds Up Your Belief Process

I achieved my unwavering belief in my future prosperity by starting with the pictures in my head. Pictures of the future me and my financial achievements. I saw them again, and again, and again. And then some more. I made them so real in my mind, that even though I was imagining the future, I made it feel like it was in the present.

As Dr. Lissa Rankin says,

Detailed visualization and affirmations help the brain imprint the new belief into the subconscious mind.

So I go *all out* when I visualize. Like, super detailed and big. I act like a kid and use my imagination... no limits. Literally *none*. I *imagine* that all the prosperity I want is already mine. I imagine how awesome it'd be to have what I want, right now. And I say, THANK YOU, over and over and over, *as if* it has already happened.

And what happens when I open my eyes after visualizing, and I look around and see that I'm not actually living in that future reality yet? Do I get discouraged? *Not on your life*. I smile big. Because I can see what's coming. I'm patient, and I'm determined. And besides, the journey is half the fun. *Bring it on, baby*.

BIG PICTURE: It's one thing to say, *"I am worthy."* It's a completely different thing to say it, and then *imagine it vividly*, in full color and using all of your senses. Because your full-sensory details carry more emotion, more brain activity, and these make your dreamy future feel more real. Which, in turn, makes it more... *believable*.

So when you read your Money Self-Talk scripts, you want to visualize what each line means *to you*, in vivid mental pictures. Close your eyes and see it. *Feel it*, as if you're living your dream life right now. Imagine this new, prosperous version of you, and step into those rich-ass shoes. Play that role!

Years ago, my husband and I would visit open houses in affluent neighborhoods, just to get inspired. To see the style, the custom architecture, the high-end furniture, and fun features, like wine cellars, infrared saunas, and home theaters. To imagine ourselves in that life. To give us pictures for our minds where we were literally inside a room of our future. We saturated our minds with inspiration, whether it was looking at things online or walking through an open house. We let our subconscious and conscious work together to make our dreams happen.

If you dream of having a certain job, sit down and picture yourself in that job. The building, your office or workspace, your coworkers. What do you do every day? What are your interactions with other people like?

And picture the accoutrements of your success in that job. If you want a beautiful, new car, then imagine yourself behind the wheel. How would it feel? What would it look like? Be specific. Be colorful. And have fun!

If you want to own your own company, then picture your office, your employees, the way you stand, and walk, and talk. What are you wearing? What time do you show up each day? What do you do once you're there? Imagine it all. And repeat these visions every day during something you do regularly, such as when you drink your coffee each morning, and then imagine it again as you fall asleep each night.

Can you see how doing this, over and over, starts to build a sense of possibility in your mind? Or even inevitability? An expectation?

It's as though you're giving your brain a blueprint and saying, "Go build me this, brain." And your subconscious goes to work, making it happen. Keeping you focused on the practical steps that will move you in the direction of your goals, but also operating stealthily behind the scenes, keeping your emotions aligned and your creativity focused on whatever is required to make it happen.

Getting to this state of self-belief isn't complicated, but it does take effort and consistency. You're training your brain the same way an athlete trains her body: through repetition. You want to teach your mind and body how it *feels* to be rich... *before* you're rich.

I know... WEIRD! But thinking, feeling, and visualizing will help you get there! And the more often you show up and make the effort, the faster it will happen. Your goal is to *feel* success now, even before you attain the success you desire. Find happy feelings, now, and watch how it can supercharge your focus, attention, effort, and ultimately, the attainment of your goals.

And guess what? Self-talk helps you get there.

Be a Commercial to Yourself

Some of the things I write in my Money Self-Talk would seem outlandish to some people. Honestly, they seemed outlandish even to me when I first wrote them. But here's the cool thing about belief: *The more often you're exposed to something, the more natural it feels to believe it.*

This applies to all kinds of things. Conspiracy theories, for instance. Or consider commercials. The more often you see an ad, the more likely you are to believe the message and buy the product. Well, you can take advantage of this phenomenon, make it work to your benefit. Simply create a commercial in your mind about the new prosperous you, and replay it over and over in your imagination.

Repeat to believe. Repeat to believe.
The more you think it and feel it, the more you believe it.

How often *you choose* to show up to your life and do your self-talk will make a big difference in how quickly you manifest your dreams.

Let me ask you this... if you wanted to write a book, and you wrote for three hours every Sunday, will you finish writing the book as quickly as if you wrote three hours every day? No! **That's the power of frequency:** The more often you show up to do something, the faster you change your brain, and the better and faster the results. This isn't just speculation. According to a study by Christopher Cascio at the University of Pennsylvania, MRI scans show that repeating affirmations may produce physical changes in the brain that amplify related neural pathways.

The New You

And when you start to believe in your dreams, something else incredible happens. *You show up to your life vastly different.* You stand tall and strong amidst any circumstances in your life. You walk differently. You respond differently. You live differently! Because you possess a core belief that everything works in your favor. If something doesn't go the way you planned, you don't mind. You just shrug. Sometimes you even laugh in the face of adversity, because you're a totally new person with a totally new rockstar brain and view of the world.

Things can happen in life, but you don't tuck your tail between your legs. You don't give in to any fears that may arise. As Paul Coelho wrote in *The Alchemist, "Don't give into your fears. If you do, you won't be able to talk to your heart."* Giving up is like a roadblock to your soul, yellow police tape—*DO NOT CROSS!* But that's not you anymore. The new you is bigger than your fears. You blast right through them, because you are capable, unstoppable, and amazing.

Money Self-Talk Script

I believe in me. I believe in my dreams. I believe in my destiny.

I deserve the most magical and prosperous life. I feel amazing.

I am brave. I am focused. And I love waking up every morning to make my dreams come true.

I have the power to be prosperous, and I see the positive in every financial situation. I am capable.

My belief is where I draw my power. My belief in me fuels my energy.

Doing what I love opens my bliss channels. Miracles follow me wherever I go.

Money is always coming to me. In all forms, flavors, and ways. From cash, to credit card rewards, to gifts. Money and I are partners!

I believe in my prosperity, and I believe in me. I have what it takes to make my dreams come true. I'm strong, confident, and resilient.

Repetition, resilience, and showing up every day like I mean it... that's how I build belief in my bones.

My performance improves under pressure. I'm classy and courageous when the chips are down.

I'm playfully outrageous!

I know I have everything I need within me, right now. It starts with my magical mindset.

I wake up in the morning looking forward to my day with excitement and appreciation. Where my energy goes, my life flows.

I elevate myself and live with an incredible mindset about abundance, prosperity, and money.

I keep going. I keep growing. I keep moving. I keep grooving. I keep dancing. I keep laughing. I love it all!

Exercises

What are your financial goals? Think of the end game here, and list the things you want to manifest, whether it's a certain career, or a lifestyle, or a specific amount of money in the bank. Does your list include a ranch in Montana? A sailboat in the Caribbean? Going back to school? Learning something cool? Starting a charitable foundation? Leaving money to your heirs? Imagine your pen is a magic wand, and you can write anything and everything you want financially.

After you've written the list, read through it three times. Then, close your eyes and visualize yourself living this dream. See your success inside your brain. There is no need to wonder how it will happen right now... this is not a planning exercise, it's a brain-training exercise. Just visualize that the end goal has already happened, and you are at the end result, successful with your dreams having come true.

You will feel excited when you do this exercise because it's pure fun and imagination. It feels good to imagine success. If you find yourself worrying about the "how," don't worry, just ignore it, and get back to those epic dreams. Repeat this exercise as often as you want, even daily.

CHAPTER 7

MONEY'S IMPORTANT MEANING

In terms of happiness, a recent estimate placed the monetary value of a small reduction in trait neuroticism (a propensity for negative moods, stress, and worry) as equivalent to an extra $314,000 income per year.

— CHRISTIAN JARRETT

To begin your epic money adventure, you must decide what money means to you and why. Because, whether it's money in your bank account, a new car, travel, a retirement account, or your stock portfolio, understanding your relationship with money helps you paint better pictures in your mind, which strengthens your belief, which makes the wealth easier to achieve.

Side note: In case you need to hear this... it's entirely acceptable to want tons of money. You have the right to want as much abundance as you desire. It doesn't matter what your mother thinks about money, or your coworkers, or your fellow parishioners. You have the right to live your most magical life, and if that means tons of cold hard cash, then go for it! And what you do with your money is your own damn business!

When you think about what money means to you, consider your views, your history, and how money was used when you were growing up. When I was a kid, my mom carried an air about her that was all champagne and diamonds, but there were also times where we lived paycheck to paycheck. My parents divorced when I was very young, and finances were not always reliable. At one point, desperate to pay the bills, my mom started a company that delivered new tires to semi-trucks, of all things. This was in the 1980s, when single women didn't have truck tire companies!

There were exciting moments, and there were extremely stressful moments, as she weathered the ups and downs of running a small business. This stressful existence got wired into my brain, and I carried the resulting scarcity-based feelings and habits into my adult life.

I would freak out when it came time to pay bills. I'd have crying fits, and I yelled a lot. I used to feel knots in my stomach and so much stress about money that I couldn't see straight. I couldn't see all the potential inside me and the opportunities around me.

But not anymore. Today, thanks to my self-talk, I have a new mind.

I'm *waaay* more relaxed around money, because I have new tools for financial success, like my mindset.

Now, my mind defaults to a more cool, calm, and strategic operator. I can still have occasional bumps in the road, but I get back up faster and smarter each time. I fall back on my mental training—my Money Self-Talk—not the negative money mindset I grew up with.

By identifying your current money mindset, and where it came from, you can more quickly replace it using Money Self-Talk, to switch your brain's direction and get it working toward building your wealth and prosperity.

Digging Into Your Soul: What Does Money Mean to You?

When I dug deep into my soul, I realized that, for me, money means freedom. It means having the freedom to choose my schedule and what projects I work on. Freedom to travel whenever I want. Freedom to go to bed and wake up when I want. Freedom to choose the doctors I want. Freedom means *having choices*, and money supports this freedom.

Money is also a solution to me, as it's much easier to solve problems when you have a lot of money. Money is play and enjoyment, and I love high-quality things. And money is contribution so I can help others. When I have more money, I can help more people.

Now It's Your Turn

So, what do *you* think about money? What are your beliefs about wealth? What are your beliefs about wealthy people? Where did those beliefs come from? What stories do you tell yourself about money? What voices from others have been getting playtime in your brain until now? Do you feel worthy of prosperity? Do you think you can only be happy once your debt is paid? Once you retire? Once you own a house? A boat? An island?

To help you dig deep and discover everything that money means to you, start by answering the following list of questions (spaces are provided at the end of this chapter):

- *Why do you want more money?*
- *How much money is "enough"?*
- *How would having more money change your life?*
- *How much does status play a role in your desire for wealth?*
- *How much does security play a role?*
- *How much does the desire for freedom play a role?*

Answering questions like these helps give you clarity and changes your focus, allowing you to make better decisions and start seeing new possibilities on the horizon. Nailing down exactly what money means to you allows you to be more authentic when it comes to money, which strengthens your belief in yourself and what's possible.

Why This Matters

It allows you to deal with fears you might have surrounding money, including any *money blocks* you carry.

I carried some serious money blocks... beliefs that were holding me back. Today, I have very different feelings about money. Previously, there always lingered a deep, hidden fear behind my desire for money. I later learned that this fear came from my underlying lack of self-worth and self-love. But back then, I didn't realize this. It was completely hidden. In fact, I thought I loved myself plenty. But I wasn't asking myself the right questions. And I wasn't being honest with myself.

I look back now though and see it all so clearly.

(I do a deep dive into self-love, and fixing those problems, in my book, *Lipstick Self-Talk: A Radical Little Self-Love Book*, but suffice it to say, self-love issues explain so much about my excessive spending and slow financial progress in my twenties and thirties.)

Here's the main thing to understand: Self-love and self-worth will *always* be the backbone of any success you have with money, love, or health. Success doesn't just mean having money, it means *feeling whole*. It's easy to find examples of millionaires—and even billionaires—who, despite having more money than they could ever spend, it's *still not enough*. They are not at peace. For them, no amount of money will ever be enough, because it's not about the money... it's about trying to fill a bottomless hole in their hearts. Without self-love, it's impossible to be truly successful (i.e. *happy*), no matter how much money you have.

So it's no surprise that I had such a dramatic turnaround in my prosperity... once I boosted my feelings of self-worth with my self-talk.

If you have money blocks, such as from fear, or lack of self-worth, it's time to *release that shit*. Once you identify any beliefs, memories, or experiences that are holding you back when it comes to money, it's time to douse those mental blocks with a firehose. Flush those feelings out of your system. *Are there any money-related things from your past that you've not forgiven yourself for?* An unwise expenditure? A bad investment? A bankruptcy? Forgive and flush! *Whoooosh!*

Really, imagine this: Line up those money blocks in your mind, grab that firehose and flush them out, all the while reciting the words:

> *I am worthy.*
> *I am worthy.*
> *I am worthy.*

The Shiny New Money-You

Once you've firehosed any old, useless, limited beliefs, it's time for fun. Now you get to explore who you *really* want to be when it comes to money.

How do you do this? By choosing your new self-image.

Think of it like Julia Roberts in *Pretty Woman*, and you're in the fancy clothing store where everybody brings you all these wonderful new outfits to try on. That's what you get to do, right now, in deciding your new money self-image: try on different images in your mind.

Try on some of these images, for instance:

"My Needs Are Met" – You've got enough money that you and your family will be financially secure, regardless of what happens (the economy, your job, healthcare needs, etc.).

The Jet Setter – You live a lavish lifestyle of extravagance, taking glamorous vacations and mingling with the rich and famous.

The "Millionaire Next Door" – You drive a modest car and live a simple life in a nice, quiet neighborhood... but you've got a few million bucks tucked away in your retirement fund. Perhaps you'll buy a second home someplace that you currently love to visit.

The Philanthropist – You see money as a means to make the world a better place, and you use your money to have the greatest positive impact that you can.

The Artist – Money provides you with the means to spend time doing what you truly love, whatever that may be... writing, making music, poetry, painting, gardening, etc.

The Adventurer – You have the freedom to explore the world, experience new cultures, and spend much of your free time in nature, exercising in fun, exciting ways.

The Entrepreneur – You're passionate about building something, and that thing has made you incredibly wealthy... but that's just a nice side benefit. You love your work so much that you don't even consider it to be work.

The Investor – You use your money to do what you love: make more money. You see an opportunity, and you pounce. It's like a game to you, and you're very good at it.

Any others? This is just a partial list out of a hundred different ways that a person might imagine financial freedom. (Write your own in the space provided at the end of this chapter.)

Be honest about your priorities and what you want. And don't be shy. It's time to decide that *this is the new you.* You decide that you're successful—and what precisely that word means to you—because most of the people who are successful *decided* they would be. They made that choice, and now you're choosing, too. You own that power in your brain.

It's time to take a big, cleansing breath, with your eyes on the prize of your future.

So... in that future, what do *you* look like?

- What are you wearing?
- How do you feel when you wake up in the morning... prosperous, and full of energy to go after your goals?
- How do you stand? How do you walk?
- What do you eat?
- What kind of car do you drive?
- What does your house look like?
- Why do you smile so much?
- How much free time do you have?
- What do you do during this free time?
- What incredible things and experiences light you up?
- What do you want when it comes to your finances?
- What is your self-image like as a wealthy person?

To be transformed, the whole basis of your thoughts must change. But your thoughts cannot change unless you have new ideas, for you think from your ideas. All transformation begins with an intense, burning desire to be transformed.

— NEVILLE GODDARD

Money Self-Talk Script

I feel big! I feel freedom! I am expansive, and I use money to create the most beautiful life ever.

I have a curious mind, and it's open for new ideas all the time. Magical, golden, shimmering ideas that glitter and catch my twinkling eyes.

Only greatness lies before me.

It is safe to follow my truth. My heart is safe. All is magically and wonderfully well! Abundance is all around me.

I am transforming, growing, and glowing anew. If I see a money block, I simply bid it adieu.

I'm calm when it comes to money, because I know I'm the master conductor of my life.

I am more than enough, and every aspect of my life is easy-breezy and fun.

I attract an overflow of money, so much money, and I am living the dream life of my design.

I get to decide money's meaning for me, and it means _____.

I am a perfect vibrational match for my desired outcome. My today is bright with anticipation, because I am worthy of my desires.

Money is unlimited. There are infinite ways to create more! I sit here right now and feel my vibe bringing more and more to me.

I am ready to share with the world. I'm excited for everything that money can do for me and my dreams.

Anything I want, I make sure I have elevated energy and confidence around those thoughts. Because I can! Because I'm worthy.

Money is a consistent, reliable part of my life.

I am going after it! I am making it happen! Prosperity and Joy and Fun, here I come!

Exercises

Describe your image of being wealthy. What does it mean to you?

Specifically, why do you want more money?

How would having more money change your life?

How much money is "enough"?

How much does status play a role in your desire for wealth?

How much does security play a role?

How much does the desire for freedom play a role?

CHAPTER 8

GET HAPPY BEFORE YOU
GET RICH

Success is not the key to happiness. Happiness is the key to success.

— ALBERT SCHWEITZER

One of the *most* important things I can say about the process of building prosperity is this:

You must find your happy *now*,
in order to make it **waaaay** easier to reach your goals.

Sure, it can be easy to imagine feeling happiness after you finally attain your prosperity goals. But the rule of this game is that you want to find happiness—*today*—and use that mental state to help draw your prosperity to you.

It seems backwards, right?

It's not.

No matter what you set out to do—athletics, academics, romance, career, raising a family, starting a business—your emotional state...

your *vibe*... is perhaps the single most important factor in determining whether you'll succeed, and how long it will take.

With this in mind, it makes perfect sense to dial in your emotional state *at the beginning*. How can you attract prosperity if you don't emit a prosperity-drawing vibe? Elevated emotions motivate you to start, work hard, bounce back from setbacks, get noticed by others, and build mutually beneficial career and business relationships. Elevated emotions create expansive thinking, and they open your eyes to opportunities around you that you can't see if you're sad or anxious. Or if you do see them, you don't seize the moment and take action.

That was exactly my experience.

When I was in debt, before I knew the magic of my mindset, I was scared, and anxious, and stressed... *for years!* Think about that... *years and years* of wasted time, when I could have been plowing forward, making steady progress, or occasional huge leaps forward, instead of wallowing in fear. But when I learned about the power of changing my mindset, and I used my self-talk to do that... whoa baby, *look out!*

I actually became happier... *in spite of* the debt. Yes, it's true. I remember so clearly a moment when I was in Italy, walking my usual three-mile trek around the rim of our town, and even though I owed $100,000 on credit cards, I had a moment where I felt such pure joy and love and awe and excitement... for life, for me, for my family, for my future, for everything. The feeling took over my body, and if anyone would've seen me, they might have said I was glowing.

It. Was. Amazing.

And this moment stood out to me so strongly *because absolutely nothing had changed about my circumstances.* I hadn't received good news. I hadn't won the lottery. I hadn't had a flash of insight and come up with an idea to solve my financial problems.

I hadn't done anything in particular, other than to read, learn, and discover from experts one particular piece of knowledge: *I would have to feel elevated emotions (happiness, awe, love, abundance) in order to bring more of those into my life.*

I had been regularly working on my self-talk and mindset for a while. And once I learned this one little idea, one day, the joy gushed out of me, all at once, taking over my mind and soul in an instant.

My life would never be the same.

And then I started to attain my prosperity goals much faster. I had already been blogging about my intentions, as I've mentioned, going so far as to publicly proclaim "I will become a millionaire" on my blog, when I still had the $100K in debt, with no freakin' idea how I'd pull off such a bold feat. But stating it publicly put a stake in the ground, a stake that, no doubt, my subconscious noticed, and this internalized belief in my eventual success caused me to take specific steps that ended up generating a small fortune.

The particular details of how I earned my wealth aren't actually what's important, as everyone's situation is different, and what I did might not work for you. But what is important is that my energy and spirit caused me to *keep trying things* until something worked. As my mom used to say, *Throw enough shit against the wall, and something will stick.*

In my case, it prompted me to start writing fiction. I wrote *furiously.* I was on a mission, and I banged out ten romance novels in a year.

Did these novels strike gold? Did they make me rich?

Actually, no. But during the process, I maintained two killer attitudes:

1. Always try new things
2. *Never give up!*

With my spirits buoyed by these two motivators, I took a course in online advertising. I ran a bunch of ads promoting the novels.

Did that work?

Well, er.... no. Not yet, anyway, haha!

But... guess what? During the process, I learned how to run ads. And then, almost on a lark, I tried running one *teeeensy* little test ad on a cute little self-help book I'd published a few months earlier, that hadn't sold hardly any copies.

And guess what happened?

It blew the freakin' doors off!

That book, *Coffee Self-Talk*, quickly sold over a hundred thousand copies. Money started pouring in. It spawned a whole series of related books, including the one you're reading now. I eventually sold the rights to Penguin Random House, and the rest is history.

Nowhere in any of that did I have any freaking clue *what would actually work*. Many of the things I thought would work didn't. And one thing I didn't expect to work—but I tried it anyway—ended up exceeding my wildest expectations. The Universe is funny like that.

Again, my details aren't important... this book isn't about becoming a writer or learning how to advertise online. It's about a formula for *preparing your mind* and heart to receive, and giving you the courage to persevere. It takes work. It takes guts. It takes time. But by reprogramming your brain with the Money Self-Talk scripts in this book, you *can* get there.

There is a universal golden formula for success. I've already snuck it in above, but I'll say it again:

1. Always try new things
2. *Never give up!*

You can see how, statistically, this approach of never giving up must always eventually work. The trick is keeping your energy and spirits high so you don't get discouraged and quit. And that's why I emphasize dialing in your happiness first, and not waiting until after you succeed. If you wait, it may never happen.

Our greatest weakness lies in giving up. The most certain way to succeed is always to try just one more time.

— THOMAS EDISON

ZOOM OUT: So, as you can see, I did not become happy once I reached my goals; I was happy *despite* my challenging circumstances, and this positive mindset *directly caused* me to reach my goals, by motivating me to keep trying new things until something clicked.

I'll add one additional tidbit about how I was able to start finding my happy despite all the debt. And that was because *I was excited* about my goals. As I mentioned in Chapter 5, when you set goals and work toward them, it feels good and lifts your spirits. So, between my self-talk and my goals, I experienced more elevated emotions on a daily basis. This not only helped me attain my goals, it also helped me to be happy throughout the journey.

During that time, I imagined so often how it would feel to pay off my debt. I imagined myself falling to my knees in gratitude. I knew I'd feel free. But when the day actually arrived that I paid it all off, I have to say, it was a bit less climactic than I'd imagined it would be. Why was that?

Because I had already imagined it so many times in my mind. So when it finally happened, I was kind of like, "Well, duh. Of course." Yes, I was grateful and excited, but I wasn't surprised. I had long believed and known with a kind of certainty that I'd get to that point, and I had happiness and feelings of freedom swimming inside me the whole ride. When it actually happened, it was just par for the course. An obvious next step.

And this is what *you* want to do... visualize *your end state* so vividly, and thoroughly, and describe it so often, that when that day arrives, it will seem as though it was inevitable. Don't wait to be happy, *choose* to be happy *now*, and use your Money Self-Talk to do this.

Money Self-Talk Script

I love my life today, and it is wonderful.

I love myself as I am right now. I am special.

Life is a big adventure, and I love the whole ride.

I find my happy in every day, now and forever, because this helps me make my dreams come true.

Feeling great now is my new rule.

I am fully and wholly worthy of everything I dream and desire.

I love feeling happy now, because it's like rocket fuel to my money goals.

My circumstances don't need to change for me to be happy. I find my happiness no matter what's going on.

I hold the power in my own hands. The magic is in my own mind. I am in control of my reactions. I am in control of my destiny.

It doesn't matter what happens outside, I choose what happens on the inside.

Even when the sky is cloudy, I know the sun is still there, beaming bright and beautiful.

I reach my money goals faster when happiness, love, and generosity are my backdrop.

Kindness fills my heart. Awe fills my soul. Appreciation fills my mind.

Happiness is an inside job, and I love that. How lucky I am that I get to be happy just because I choose to be.

I love my life today, it is wonderful. So very, very wonderful.

Exercise

Doing your Money Self-Talk is a key to helping you attain your financial dreams, but it also helps you increase your happiness. Make a list of things you enjoy doing and that bring you pleasure.

For me, that's journaling, reading, taking walks, spending time in nature, exploring, volunteering for animal shelters, eating delicious food, doing things with my family, seeing my daughter smile, and more. Write a list for yourself, taking into consideration things that make you smile and enjoy yourself. Then, add one of the items on your list to your calendar each week, to make sure you're enjoying life on your road to riches.

CHAPTER 9

THE MONEY TANGO

The money is already printed. You just have to go get it.

— Anonymous

There I was, sitting on the couch, binge-watching *Emily in Paris* on Netflix. I was recovering from COVID after being sick for almost a week. I'd handled the virus like a champ, nothing serious, mostly just mild flu-like symptoms. And although I'd had moments where I felt like shit, I told myself, hey, I was *sparkly shit.*

Even though my recovery was rapid, during those first few days, there I was on the couch, staring at the ceiling... staring into nothingness... and I didn't think about anything work-related. I didn't think about writing, or creating, or money in general.

Once I made it over the hump and was starting to feel a little better, I still wasn't ready to work. My brain was foggy and spacey, with zero creative connections or inspiration. The thought of writing a single sentence was out of the question. This annoyed me a bit because I'd spent enough time *not* working while I was sick, and the eager beaver in me started impatiently tapping her toes—*Tap! Tap! Tap! I want to write!*

And truth be told, *I wanted to make money.*

Sigh—my usually trusty creativity was not cooperating. It was as if there was a law against my body working while under any influence of COVID. But I just wasn't fully healed yet, and I began to wonder when I'd write again.

And then something happened... a scene from the TV show reminded me that I have an incredible relationship with money, and it always has my back, even when my back is laid up on the couch, nowhere near a laptop.

The scene was when Emily, a workaholic by European standards, was in St. Tropez. It was the weekend, and she was trying to do some work, of course. But any European coworker she called to ask questions kept telling her, *"It is zeh weekend. You are not allowed to work. It is zeh law."*

And in this moment, a spark of realization glittered through me. The French do not work on the weekend, and yet they are still worthy of their compensation. And I remembered how I, too, am worthy of money even though I was not working right then. Money and I are partners. We tango together. Sometimes I take the lead, and sometimes money takes the lead.

You see... in the past, before my magical-self-talk life, I operated strictly under a pay-for-performance mentality. If I'd been sick on the couch, I would've been jumping out of my skin to work from the second my butt hit the cushion. Out of fear, of course. I'd have been barking orders at everyone to do things if I couldn't myself. Thankfully, I've come a long way, and this experience was different. So although I did get a few ants in my pants, I course corrected. Thanks to *Emily in Paris.*

In that moment, I kicked my feet back up and chilled out. I knew that I was worthy of money coming to me, whether I was sleeping or sick or playing and having a good time. Because that's my tango with money. That's my magical mindset about money. That's the job I gave it in our relationship: Money comes to me, even when I'm not directly working. It might be weird to foster this relationship with money, but that's what I do. Money and I each pulled up a chair to the table and became partners in my mind. And that's one of the most important things I did when it came to prosperity... I entered into a formal relationship with money. You might even call it *intimate*. Yes, I've blown kisses to my money.

And that's exactly what was happening in real time. While I snoozed between Netflix episodes, our products continued to sell, advertising was cheap... and I wasn't doing a damn thing. Or was I? I might not have been working directly on a project, but I was always keeping my money mind strong with affirmations and feelings of worthiness. Like Margaret Thatcher said, *"I wasn't lucky. I deserved it."*

Because I'm worthy. (We all are.) Because money and I are partners. And even if I'm down temporarily, money keeps coming to me. Always. Always. Always. *That's my mindset. That's my energy.*

Money Self-Talk Script

Money and I have the most brilliant relationship. We take care of one another.

I love my relationship with money, and I honor it. Thank you, money.

I am worthy of money, and I am worthy of being in a fabulous relationship with it. We love each other.

Money is always coming to me, in a million different ways. I just need to open my arms and run toward it like reunited lovers.

I am so grateful for the money I have at this very second, no matter what the amount is, and for all the money coming to me in the future.

I am grateful for everything in my life right now: food, water, shelter, health, family, love, the sun, moon, and stars... and shoes!

Money supports me, and I take excellent care of my money.

I magnetize success into my world with confidence and conviction. I easily attract those who need what I have to give.

I have a huge, kind heart, and it makes me want to do so much good in the world with my money.

I am deserving of everything I want. We all are.

Thank you for my wealth. Thank you for my money. Thank you for everything. Thank you, thank you, thank you.

There is always more than enough for me. I am loved deeply, appreciated wholly, and supported completely by money. I am full of love, and I am loved.

I am filled with peace about my relationship with money. We are a phenomenal team.

I conduct myself from a beautifully elevated state, viewing myself as abundant, worthy, and wealthy.

I vibrate at a high level, smiling as I flow through my day, having the time of my life.

Exercise

Imagine you're sitting at a table. Across from you on the table sits a big stack of money, and it's listening. Waiting. Eager to help you.

It's time to set this relationship straight. What is your relationship with money going to be like? What is money's job? How is it going to help you? Are you in charge of it, or vice versa? (Hint: You're in charge.) Imagine you're hiring money, and you get to set the terms. Write down a few sentences describing your relationship with money, and how it's going to help you reach your goals.

CHAPTER 10

WAYS TO MORE MONEY

Do what you love. Know your own bone; gnaw at it, bury it, unearth it, and gnaw it still.

— HENRY DAVID THOREAU

In Chapter 2, I discussed the difference between what I call the "practical" and the "magical" when it comes to money. In this chapter, we're going to go deeper into both of them.

Magical Ways to More Money

Money can come to you in many ways, from career advancements, to a free dinner, to holiday gifts, and each source of money deserves its own splash of gratitude. So when you embark on this new prosperity adventure, I want you to start paying attention to the many ways that abundance comes to you. *Because it all counts.* And the more times you notice and feel grateful for this stuff, the more you'll likely end up seeing more, more, and more.

Money could be an unexpected check or refund. It could be someone buying you coffee or lunch. It can be rewards on a credit card or a birthday gift. Or maybe a sudden discount on an item you weren't expecting. Maybe you get a raise. Maybe someone leaves you money in a will, or you win a prize, like a trip, cash, or an appliance. Money comes in many forms, and when you recognize this, you realize how much more abundance you actually have, which lifts your spirits, which then opens your eyes to even more. *It all adds up!* And I think of these as magical because they *feel* magical.

When we lived in Italy, every other day, our landlord brought us a bounty of produce from his garden and olive oil from his orchard. He'd ring the doorbell, and I'd open it to find him standing there, a sprightly eighty years old, blue eyes twinkling, as he handed me a basket filled with a colorful assortment of squash blossoms, grapes, potatoes, fresh figs, and so much more, depending on the season. I was so grateful every time, and it touched me deeply in my soul as I gave thanks to him and then gave thanks to the abundance of the universe.

It didn't escape me that these gifts were saving me from spending money on produce, and that was a form of money coming to me. But the bigger gift was the love and friendship, the kind gesture, and the special magic of eating food that he grew on land that he worked with his own hands. It was a truly special gift, every time, and a frequent reminder that abundance often comes in forms other than money.

I could go on and on with examples, but the point is for you to be on the lookout for unexpected gifts that appear in your own life, both monetary and otherwise.

Practical Ways to Receive More Money

Now let's talk about some practical ways to increase prosperity. And let's start with some inspirations about single-person businesses.

Million-Dollar Micro Businesses

In the book, *The Million-Dollar, One-Person Business,* author Elaine Pofeldt writes:

> *In 2017, there were 41,666 non-employer firms—that is, those that do not employ anyone other than the owners—that brought in between $1 million and $2,499,999 in annual revenue. In 2017, there were 2447 businesses employing only their owners they had annual receipts of $2.5 million to 4.99 million, and 420 of these brought in $5 million or more.*

The author goes on to explain that one of the factors driving the growth and sustainability of these "million-dollar micro businesses" is the internet. It's an enabler. You can now jump into a *"vast global marketplace cheaply and quickly."*

A World Without Gatekeepers

It's difficult to overstate the impact the internet has had from giving *anybody* virtually unlimited opportunity to become financially independent.

Think about it... in the past, there were *gatekeepers*—entities and individuals who had the power to choose whether or not you advance. Whether getting into a good school, getting a certain job, a promotion, a business loan, a book deal, a record deal, your own radio show, your own TV show, distribution for a product you produce... there were people at every step of the way who could say *no*.

These barriers are essentially gone in most fields now. In many ways, we now live in a *permissionless* society. You still might not get into Harvard, or Stanford, or MIT, but you *can* take any of their courses online for free. You can learn a graduate degree's worth of knowledge, sufficient to become, say, a machine learning engineer earning $300K a year... with *zero student debt.*

I say "most fields" because some domains still have gatekeepers, for good reason. Medical school, for example... you don't want just anybody doing surgery on you, ya know? But there is nobody preventing anybody from becoming an entrepreneur, freelancer, YouTuber, podcaster, Etsy creator, eBay seller, Amazon seller, or best-selling author. You can learn almost any skill online, and then turn around and sell that service to others.

I take it back, there is still one very powerful gatekeeper. One person who has the power to stop you *dead in your tracks...*

You.

Only you have the ability to prevent you from doing these things.

Of course, the market decides what it will buy, but that's no one individual, no gatekeeper. The market's influence is highly diluted, a few billion people spread around the globe. All you need to do is come up with something that a handful of them will pay for.

To be clear, I am NOT saying it's easy. It's not. If it were easy, everyone would do it. What I'm saying is that it's *doable*. Which is why thousands of people *have* done it.

You might say, *Well Kristen, not everybody can be a self-published author... there'd be too many books.* That's absolutely correct. But I'm not saying *everyone* can do this, I'm saying *anyone* can. Most people never will. It won't even cross most people's mind, as they're permanently stuck in the traditional gatekept, employer/employee worldview. And this leaves the door wide open for anybody who's willing to put in the effort.

(Note: Plenty of employed individuals can become wealthy through their jobs... skilled professionals, executives, rockstar salespeople, or through employee stock options, etc. Or even lower-paid employees, by saving and investing over the long term. And there *are* ways to become wealthy despite gatekeepers—sometimes the gatekeeper says yes—but this section serves to expand your horizons and highlight the idea that wide-open possibilities exist, even if you don't know about them yet.)

What does it mean when *you're the gatekeeper*?

It means you are the only one who can stop you from succeeding. To some, this is liberating. It means yes, you can do it... it's completely *doable*. To others, it's a little scary. It means there's no excuses, no one else to blame if it doesn't happen. It means you're responsible for your outcome... but you already knew that, right?

Whether you embrace the opportunity with excitement, or gird yourself against fear of failure, there is only one simple tool you need to remember...

Money Self-Talk.

Your self-talk is, hands-down, THE best way to build belief and motivation. To dream big. To make plans. To take action. To adapt and learn as you go. To get back up when you get knocked down. To keep on trying things. To keep on going, no matter what, and never stop until you succeed.

Use the scripts in this book. That's why they're here. And you can write your own self-talk to address your specific needs. The main thing is to just start doing it, and then keep on doing it. Show up and do the work, every day.

That's the key to succeeding in a world with no gatekeepers, where the only major hurdle is you.

Idea: Making Money By "Doing You"

I want to remind you that you are amazing. You have potential. And your uniqueness is attractive. I want you to remember that you are the *only you* out there. You come with your own style. You have your own story. And this makes you unique.

So guess what? You don't have to worry about what's already in the marketplace. Just because someone else is doing (or selling) the thing that you want to do, does not mean that you can't do it. For example, in my line of work, it doesn't matter that there are a million other authors out there. No one else writes books the way I write, with my voice, with my stories. I am unique and 100% special in that way. And so are you.

You have life experiences and a point of view that is your own, and whatever thing, product, or service that you want to sell, or whatever job you want to have, *only you can do in the way that you will do it.* Every barista makes the coffee a little bit differently. Every doctor has their own unique skills and bedside manner. So *be your truth...* because someone out there needs it.

Self-consciousness is the enemy of interestingness.

— MALCOLM GLADWELL

Get Started

Sometimes ideas and inspiration come to you as vague hunches and feelings—pay attention to these. Sometimes it's small, like an inkling. And sometimes inspiration fires in your soul, begging you to take heed. But if you don't have any ideas right now, that's cool, too. They can come out of nowhere, like a shooting star, *when you keep your mind open to them.*

In the meantime, ask yourself these questions to help you start thinking.

- What brings me so much excitement that, when I do it or think about it, I burst with rainbow energy? In other words... what's fun for me?
- What skills do I have right now?
- What new skills do I want to acquire?

- What are my strengths?
- What are my hobbies?
- What am I passionate about?
- What am I *obsessed* about?
- Write down three words that describe me. (When I thought about this for myself, I came up with: optimistic, adaptable, and tiger. Yeah, that's right, *tiger*.)
- If I had all the time in the world, what would I do?
- If I had very little time left, what would I do?

Sarah Blakely (founder of Spanx women's underwear) was selling fax machines door-to-door. One day, she thought to herself, *"I'm in the wrong movie."* The neat thing about Sarah is that she's a student of manifesting and Law-of-Attraction-type stuff. She went home that night and wrote in her journal, *"What am I good at?"* And although she knew she was good at sales, she decided, then and there, that she wanted to invent a product to sell to millions of people that would help their lives. And she asked the Universe for an idea.

It didn't happen overnight. Two years later, she came up with the idea to cut the feet off of control-top pantyhose. This one little idea started her on a new trajectory toward becoming a *billionaire*.

She asked the Universe for an idea, and she got one. Is this "Universe" stuff hokey? Divine intervention? Just planting a seed for her RAS Wizard (see Chapter 5) to be on the lookout for great ideas? I don't know. I'm not sure it matters. What matters is *that it works*.

Because Sarah knew where she wanted to end up (super rich), her brain started making a thousand little subconscious decisions all along the way that led her to come up with the idea and cut the feet off those pantyhose. If Sarah Blakely can use intuition as a guide and ask for signs... if Sarah Blakely can talk to the Universe and become a billionaire... then we're in good company!

How do you know you love something? How do you feel when you are fully expressing yourself? Learn that feeling and then start looking, not for the thing, but for the feeling.

— THE LION TRACKER'S GUIDE TO LIFE

Mine Your Mistakes

Another tip for finding ideas is to look at the mistakes and hard times in your life. There are diamonds to be found, buried in this rough terrain. When you think about your life, ponder the lessons you've learned, especially the hard lessons, the tough times, because those create valuable insights you can share with others. Perhaps there's a product you can make in there. Perhaps there's a class you can teach, or a book you can write.

Ask yourself, *"Is there something I wish I could go back and tell my past self?"*

It can be about anything: business, family, diet, fitness, health, parenting, animals, school, fixing stuff around the house... anything. Dig deep, and see if you find an intersection between something you're passionate about and a life lesson you've learned. Could you write a blog post about it? Or give a lecture? Or create a YouTube video, or share it on Instagram, or TikTok?

My mom cares for her husband with dementia, and let me tell you, she's learned a lot about the disease and the healthcare system. Stuff she really would've benefitted from knowing at the beginning. She could definitely teach a course on the subject, and anyone in the same boat would love to learn what she knows.

She's also funny as hell, and a gifted storyteller. Imagine the magic combination, offering very useful, practical advice, to people who are going through something very difficult, but in a way that makes them laugh while they're learning. Slam dunk. As the meme says, *Shut up and take my money!*

The point is, you can make a business out of teaching lessons you've learned, because there are people out there who want your tips and tricks.

Storytelling has been around since people have been around, and we all love learning from other people's stories. It's in our DNA. Hunter-gatherers used stories to teach younger people how to survive. When children were too young to join the adults on a hunt, they still needed to learn about hunting, and they learned it through stories told around the campfire. In this way, we haven't changed, and you can teach others by telling them your own story.

Neurologist and bestselling author Oliver Sacks wrote,

> *We call it storytelling. It is the great human implement that renders the world comprehensible to us and renders us comprehensible to ourselves. Its function is our shared inheritance; its form is the crucible of our difference: "Biologically, physiologically, we are not so different from each other; historically, as narratives—we are each of us unique."*

Feeling Shy

And if you feel vulnerable or shy about sharing your stories... then good. Writer Neil Gaiman says about writing:

> *The moment that you feel that, just possibly, you're walking down the street naked, exposing too much of your heart and your mind and what exists on the inside, showing too much of yourself. That's the moment you may be starting to get it right.*

Coming Up Empty?

But if you're having trouble finding past experiences to mine, then go on a *new* journey and look for any new experiences that you can learn from and teach others about later.

A few years ago, one of the ways we initially decided on to work on reducing our debt was to drastically cut our living expenses. A great way to do that was living somewhere really cheap, like outside the United States. Or by housesitting, which means living rent-free in exchange for taking care of somebody's house and pets while they are away. Or in our case, both! Housesitting in countries with cheaper living expenses, like food and healthcare. *Boom!*

Because we worked from laptops, we decided to be *digital nomads*, and we used housesitting to reduce our expenses while traveling the world. Along the way, I learned incredible lessons and tips. What did I do with this valuable information? I wrote a book about how to score the best housesits, of course! I also shared it as a topic on my blog, which had affiliate links that continue generating passive income for me even now, years later.

Skills Advantages & Partnerships

Look for opportunities where you have an advantage because of your current skills and passions. For example, my girlfriend learned how to bow hunt, and she was so inspired by it that she started her own cool t-shirt company called *Bow Bunny*.

Did she know anything about building a website, or making t-shirts, or registering a trademark? Nope! She had to learn how to do it all. She doesn't have a degree in business or design. That badass babe struck out on her own, hopped online, and started googling. Her shirts are my favorite t-shirts ever! Seriously, I own about fifteen of them. (Check out her Instagram: @bowbunnyhuntress.)

Don't Feel Like Going It Alone?

Consider people you might want to team up with. Don't reinvent the wheel if you don't have to. Got a friend or family member who's good at a skill you lack, and vice versa? Maybe join forces!

I'm a fast writer, and I can crank out 10,000 words in a day. My husband writes and has creative ideas, but he doesn't write anywhere near as fast as I do. He also excels at technology, marketing, design, spreadsheets, and foot rubs. I write while he rubs my feet... hehe, just kidding. He takes on all those other roles, and together, we make an epic publishing team.

I have another friend who fell in love with a personal trainer who specialized in exercising with a *mace* (a metal pole with a heavy metal ball on the end). One year, she wanted to surprise him for Christmas, and she went on Udemi.com to take a class on how to create a mace exercise routine. On Christmas, she turned on his favorite heavy metal music, and she performed the mace routine for her thoroughly stunned man. She might've even been wearing a Santa hat!

Well, this unusual activity turned into her passion, and she started exercising with a mace regularly for her own fitness.

And the more she did it, the more she learned. She also had a passion for nutrition, which she had studied years prior. She took her nutrition education, plus what she learned about the mace, and she combined it with her boyfriend's knowledge of mace workouts... and they started a business together. They now do online courses and workshops for this incredibly cool, unique exercise! (See RockHardAthletics.com.)

Think about your own relationships... can you partner up with an expert in something you don't know much about?

Maybe you're a good writer, and you have a friend with real estate rentals. Or maybe you know online marketing, and your sister is an amazing cook. Or maybe you have the subject matter expertise, but you need someone to take on the production stuff, like audio, video, and editing it all together into something amazing.

When you consider everything you're good at, you might discover there's an easy on-ramp to making money. And when you team up with someone else, it can get everything going even faster.

Ask yourself...

- What are topics that I could give a five-minute speech on right now?
- Are there any life lessons in my heart that I could turn into a children's book?
- What topics could I start a podcast about?
- Can I think of any one-minute videos that I could create about various topics?
- What are all the things I can give advice on?
- What new things would I like to explore and teach people about later?
- What are my friends, coworkers, and family experts in?

When you answer these questions (there are spaces at the end of this chapter), jot down *every little thing* that pops into your mind... from woodworking, to cooking chicken, to gardening, to fixing things, to the best way to shave your legs, to camping, to applying false eyelashes, to organizing your closet, to playing the piano.

And then be on the lookout for inspiration!

Carry a notebook (or use the Notes app on your phone), and whenever you see something you love, jot it down. Whenever you see something that you don't love, scribble that down, too... sometimes these inspire ways to make a better product. And when you wish you had a product that doesn't exist, write that down, too.

This habit of jotting down ideas opens your eyes, and makes you think of things more often. You never know what you'll come up with!

Money Self-Talk Script

I am filled with ideas and ways to make more money.

Prosperity is here, and opportunities and shining doors of possibilities surround me.

Everything I need is within me now. Vitality and energy flow in my veins.

My time is valuable. My energy is valuable and worth money. I am worthy of getting paid.

Money finds me in all kinds of ways.

I am calm, certain, sure, and centered about money. I know myself, I love myself, and I trust my beautiful, courageous, happy self with money.

My possibilities are infinite. I understand how money works, and I know how to make more of it anytime I want.

I am grateful for my intelligence and resourcefulness. I can do anything!

I love finding new ways to make money, and I am open to all the new ideas coming my way.

Money and I have an epic partnership. We rock!

I attract the right people, in the right place, and at the right time. I'm a magnet for success.

I allow myself to make more money, create more abundance, and attract my dream life to me.

I deserve to have the abundance I desire. I'm attracting wealth, and I keep my eyes open for the next inspiring step to take.

Thank you, life. Thank you, me. Thank you for everything I already have right now. And thank you for everything that is making its way to me. I am honored and grateful.

My goods and services are wanted and desired. I add value to the world. I love my life. I am focused on success.

Exercises

What are topics that I could give a five-minute speech on right now?

Are there any life lessons in my heart that I could turn into a children's book?

What topics could I start a podcast about?

Can I think of any one-minute videos that I could create about various topics?

What are all the things I can give advice on?

What new things would I like to explore and teach people about later?

What are my friends, coworkers, and family experts in?

CHAPTER 11

STAY OPEN

Let yourself feel happy about the abundance you will have, because it will come.

— Natalie Ledwell

When I was eleven years old, I had a massive crush on child actor Corey Haim. We were destined to be together. One summer afternoon, I sat at a little wooden table in the middle of my driveway writing a letter to him. I used my special stationary that had colorful balloons on it. In my letter, I told him how much I liked him and how wonderful I thought he was, and then I stuck it in the mail. I totally thought he was going to write back to me, properly court me, and that we'd get married someday.

I didn't marry Corey Haim.

Turns out, I got someone even better. My dream come true, the most incredible man in my life, my husband, Greg. The end goal was true love, it just didn't come in the form of Corey Haim.

After the previous chapter on practical money-making inspiration, you might have a list as long as your arm full of ideas about your future abundance. And that's fantastic.

But I need to share something with you.

It might not happen.

Wait... what?

When you do your Money Self-Talk, you come to it from a place of expansiveness, aiming for your *big end goal*: Prosperity. (In whatever form that word means for you.) The practical examples I offered for making money are nowhere near an exhaustive list; they are meant to get you thinking and start taking inspired steps. But taking steps doesn't always mean the steps you take will be the thing that leads to your golden ticket. Prosperity has a way of zigging and zagging, surprising you. Sometimes even showing up when you least expect it, despite your careful planning.

When I was living in Italy, focusing hard and visualizing having more money, I had no idea how it was going to happen. The important thing was being confident that something *would* happen. This doesn't mean you sit around doing nothing... *oh, hell no...* you take steps. *Lots* of them. *You take action!* But you don't always know which steps are going to strike gold.

Despite having no clear direction, I knew I had to take steps, I had to do something. *Anything.* So I researched all kinds of different ways to make money, from writing, to starting a drop-shipping business, I listened to podcasts, I blogged, I networked with tech entrepreneurs in Europe and online. I stayed open to hunches, and I tried different things, because the road ahead only appears when you're moving forward. You take a first step to start the process. It's like those moving sidewalks at airports... it only starts moving you to your destination once you take action and step onto it.

Well, I got it into my mind that the solution for making money would be Greg writing sci-fi novels, something he'd pondered for years. We talked about it a lot, so I naturally imagined his writing would be our ticket to prosperity... not just the writing, but also because he's got the marketing chops to potentially break out from a crowded field. Who knows... maybe bestseller lists and even movie deals! I also visualized our prosperity *end goal*: owning our own home, bills paid off, and a pile of money in a Vanguard account.

I visualized that juicy life all day long.

Well, what happened?

A year later, *I was the one writing novels.* Romance novels, actually, under the pen name Brisa Starr. Not in my wildest dreams had I planned for that! Except that I'd dropped some self-talk into my Coffee Self-Talk scripts about me being a "creative and a prolific writer" (I had a blog at the time, so I was always writing something). But those sneaky little planted seeds manifested in a way I never dreamed, literally delivering fully formed fiction stories to my brain, ready to be put down on paper.

Which I promptly did, writing my first novel in a month. And then another, and then another. And as I mentioned previously, even these were not what created the wealth... it was the marketing tactics we learned in the process, which we applied to a completely different type of book.

So, you can see how far my outcome strayed from my original plan. Was the plan wasted? No! It launched me in directions that—with zigs and zags—got me to my debt-free, house-owning picture of prosperity. Each step was a causal link from the previous. If we hadn't been marinating in the idea of writing sci-fi novels, I don't think the idea of romance novels would have come to mind. If I hadn't been writing romance novels, we wouldn't have learned how to do advertising. Without ads, it's doubtful that Coffee Self-Talk would have become an international bestseller.

Why This Matters

This is just my story, but if you ask around to rich people you know, you'll often find the exact same pattern: motion → zigzags (or *pivots*, as tech founders call it) → success.

Steve Jobs famously came up for the idea of using fonts on the original Macintosh computer because he had taken a calligraphy course "just for fun." By adding fonts and a graphical user interface, he launched the desktop publishing revolution, and the rest is Apple history.

You just never know where things are going to lead. Instead of letting this natural uncertainty freak you out, you must embrace it, and dive in head first. Take those initial steps! Don't worry what happens next, you'll figure out the rest later!

Just because you take steps in one direction toward your prosperity goal doesn't mean you won't end up going in a wildly different direction before you get there. And that's where the importance of *staying open* comes into play. Don't be so tunnel-visioned that you don't entertain other options. The universe will show you all kinds of things.

Surrender to Uncertainty

Think of it in terms of *surrendering*. You read your Money Self-Talk scripts, you think about ways to attain your goals, you put out your beautiful vibration, and you start seeing things that seem to magically line up to help you. Even though you take steps in a certain direction, you also surrender to other possibilities.

You relax.

You unfold and allow.

You surrender to the whole epic process.

As Maxwell Maltz writes in the classic book, *PsychoCybernetics,*

> *The means by which your success mechanism works often take care of themselves and do so effortlessly when you supply the goal to your brain. The precise action steps will come to you without stress, tension, or worry about how you are going to accomplish the results you seek... After you formed a mental image of the goal you seek to create, the hows will come to you, not before. Remain calm and relaxed, and the answers will arrive.*

Phew! Right?

Isn't it a relief that you don't need to have everything figured out all the time? There's a magical dance between the *known* and the *unknown,* and the sooner you get comfortable with this way the Universe dances, the more relaxed you feel through the entire journey. Relaxation is an elevated state that helps you see more opportunities. But if you have too many "hows" squirreling through your mind, they can create one-track thinking and make it difficult to see unexpected alternatives.

Instead of asking *how,* say to yourself...

> *Money is coming somehow.*
> *I might not know how,*
> *right now,*
> *but I know it will,*
> *because I'm worthy.*

Personally, I follow an *ebb and flow* pattern for most of my manifesting. First, I get all fired up and make plans and goals... that's the practical part of me. Then, I focus on them and take steps (more practical). But then, I let go. I let go of outcomes for how I think it's supposed to work... that's the magical part.

Strangely enough, it's often during this time of relaxation and surrender that I get my biggest ideas, and they're totally different and unexpected!

You want your *subconscious* mind to be working on helping you reach your goals. In fact, a former chief of research at General Electric once said that most of his discoveries came as hunches during a period of relaxing, which came after a period of intensive thinking.

> *We're lost, but we're making good time.*
>
> — YOGI BERRA

Money Self-Talk Script

Money is coming to me. I might not know how right now, but I know it will, because I'm worthy.

I stay open to the unknown, the unexpected, and I welcome the magic that's there.

I am lit up today! Woohoo! I am bouncing on the stars! I swing from the sun. My positive, confident attitude finds yeses around every corner.

I get to decide how I respond to anything and everything, and I always see the silver lining.

I stay calm, no matter what is going on around me. I surrender to the magic.

I smile and wink at myself in the mirror because I know amazing synchronicities happen all the time for me.

I flow through my day, dancing and having fun, and money flows to me from up, down, and all around.

Money is coming to me. I might not know how right now, but I know it will, because I'm worthy.

I love life, and life loves me. I love abundance, and abundance loves me.

I am relaxed and happy. I open my mind to all the possibilities.

I am grateful that I am financially abundant, and that prosperity is all around me.

I am happy, strong, and smart. I am happy, strong, and smart. I am happy, strong, and smart.

I allow myself to dream and float on the breeze. I am open to new ideas, and they seek me.

I am resilient in the face of stress. I am capable. I am strong.

Money is coming to me. I might not know how right now, but I know it will, because I'm worthy.

Exercises

Do you have any goals that you're hesitant to pursue because of fear or self-doubt? If so, how can you reframe any failures as simply learning opportunities on your path to success?

What are three small, simple steps you can take to start making progress toward this goal?

CHAPTER 12

YOUR PROSPERITY ENVIRONMENT

See yourself living in abundance, and you will attract it. It always works, it works every time with every person.

— BOB PROCTOR

Did you know that your physical environment can affect your success? According to Lindsay T. Graham, PhD, at the Center for the Built Environment at UC Berkeley,

> *Our homes can be incredibly important tools for shaping our daily experiences. How they're organized, decorated, and furnished can be curated to evoke a varied palette of feelings and serve as a form of emotional regulation.*

By surrounding yourself with inspiring, pretty, or cool things, you impact your energy, emotions, and feelings. And by now, you know how important your vibe is for increasing your wealth. You want the places where you spend the most time to inspire your greatest money mindset.

Step 1: Determine Your Environment

Decide what comprises your work environment. Is it your office? Your entire house? Maybe just your desk? Or perhaps it's your car, if you spend a lot of time on the road or drive clients around much. Do you ever set up shop with your laptop at Starbucks?

Step 2: Declutter

To properly design the most magnificent workspace, you need a sense of openness to work with, like a blank canvas. In order to do this, you must declutter. And you might as well clean while you're at it. Make sure you don't have piles of stuff all over your desk, or a bunch of crumbs and trash in your car. Whatever place you're going to make as your money-manifesting environment, make sure it's as clean and spacious as possible.

Step 3: Design Time

Once you've got your blank canvas, it's design time! To begin, think about things that bring you joy, or make you feel appreciated. Or consider things that, when you see them, you're dumbstruck for a moment because of their beauty, and awe washes through you. I feel this way about crystals, candles, fresh flowers, old books from the 1920s, '30s and '40s. Oh, and stacks of cash. :)

On my desk, I have things that reflect beauty, creativity, and relaxation, and even a sense of opulence. My lamp, for example, has beautiful, crystal fringe-thingies hanging from the lampshade. Although the lamp didn't cost much, it looks like it did, and I feel rich when I look at it. I also like candles, salt lamps, and crystals (citrine, amethyst, quartz, etc.). They add a tinge of mysticism to my day, and this helps especially when I write fiction.

I'm also a lover of fountain pens. They harken back to a different time, and when I'm using one, I feel like I'm transporting myself into the past. I surround myself with books, too, and I always have easy access to a whiteboard and beautiful pads of paper for jotting down ideas.

I keep a stash of Bala exercise bars and weights next to my desk. Every hour, my alarm reminds me to get up to move around, do some squats, or bang out a set of bicep curls. It's also important to have ergonomic comfort with your chair and desk... this is not a place to skimp. I like to toggle between standing and sitting, so I bought a desk that quietly raises and lowers with the push of a button. This may seem like a luxury to some, but it's much healthier than sitting for hours at a time.

And last but not least, I literally have a stack of hundred-dollar bills on my desk. It started with $20 bills, and I later graduated to hundred-dollar bills... just there for me to see. Weird, right? Maybe, but *seeing them makes me feel rich*. (Of course, my office is a private home office. If I worked around other people, I wouldn't keep a stack of cold, hard, sexy cash just sittin' there.)

So, what kinds of things inspire you and why?

Is it a particular piece of art? A certain color? Technology? Action figures? Something from your childhood? According to James Clear, author of *Atomic Habits*,

> *Our behavior is not defined by the object in the environment, but by our relationship to them. Stop thinking about your environment as filled with objects, and start thinking about it as filled with relationships.*

Designing your space goes beyond physical objects, however. Sound, for instance. Are there loud noises around your office? If you work at home, is the TV always on and distracting you?

Or perhaps you share a space, either at home or elsewhere. If so, consider purchasing a room divider to carve out some private space for yourself. When we lived in Italy, my husband, daughter, and I all shared one office. And while it was great to share energy when working on something, there were times I wanted privacy. A room divider is an easy way to do that. And if you constantly hear distracting noise, consider investing in a good pair of noise-canceling headphones.

If you're fortunate enough to have a window near you, then congratulations! That's something to celebrate. Windows allow you to see outside, ideally see some nature, and let your mind wander creatively, or give your eyes a break from staring at a computer display. If you don't have a window, or if your view isn't good, then consider bringing plants into your environment. Plants are a simple but powerful way to create a beautiful, healthy vibe.

And don't forget your sense of smell! Scents can have powerful psychological effects. Some inspiring smells for your work environment could be mint, lemon, and rosemary essential oils. Or fresh brewed coffee! Peppermint wakes me up, and rosemary is reputed to be good for memory. Lemon has benefits, too. In one study, researchers in Japan found that typing mistakes dropped by 54% when lemon scent was added to a workplace!

Mind-Body-Soul Environment

There's another environment we need to address: your *mind-body-soul*.

Mind: Negative Self-Talk

When it comes to decluttering, be ruthless at getting rid of any negative self-beliefs that are taking up space in your *mental environment*. Make a commitment to yourself, right now, that you are unavailable for any negative, downer thinking, because negative self-beliefs can have a profound effect and set you back, not just in your quest for financial abundance, but in all areas of your life.

Body: Lipstick and Suits

A great way to improve your body's "environment" is to dress for success. Some of my best days happen when I wear shimmering pink lipstick, and my hair looks good. Or when I'm wearing my favorite jeans or a cool pair of shoes that make me smile. For you, it might be a suit or high heels.

If you imbue an article of clothing or jewelry with special meaning, it can have a powerful effect on your mental state, like a talisman. All you have to do is state, "This is my [goal] [article of clothing or accessory]." For instance, your "writer's hat" or your "millionaire watch."

When my husband was an undergrad, he had a goal of going to graduate school at Harvard. He had a special pair of socks—his "Harvard socks"—that he always wore when taking an exam. It wasn't a superstition, it was a tangible reminder of his long-term goal, and putting them on before a test became a trigger to his brain to focus.

In another example, a student who wanted to go to medical school would wear a white doctor's coat and stethoscope while studying! Can you imagine the message that pounds into your subconscious? *Dress for success.* Dress as the person you want to become. Act *as if.*

Soul: Scarring Grudges

Last but not least, let's talk about decluttering the environment of your *soul.* Are you holding on to any grudges? Is there someone you haven't forgiven? Are you holding on to old, crappy beliefs about you or life? If so, drop them like a handful of burning rocks. You *must* change *all* that. You must forgive, move on, and clear the decks of your soul, in order to have a sparkly clean vibration. That's how you elevate your energy more, to make it easier to attract money.

Money Self-Talk Script

Abundance, money, and gargantuan compensation are coming to me, today and every day. Even while I sleep. My life is easy like that.

I am the hero of my own financial wellness.

Surrounding myself with inspiring things makes a significant difference in my manifesting ability.

I go from success, to success, to success. I have a Mega-Midas touch.

I'm slaying it! I'm the boss of my life. I'm in awe and excited. I'm flexing my prosperity muscles. Bam!

I surround myself with success and meaningful items that inspire me. I am worth it.

It's easy for me to let go of grudges. It's easy for me to forgive.

I keep my vibe sparkly and buffed to a shine by loving myself and appreciating my amazing life.

I let go of anything that doesn't boost my happiness. I learn and dance on happily.

I believe. I believe. I believe. I believe in me.

My environment beautifully supports my work and my ability to manifest my dreams.

I keep my mind on the goal, on the feeling of success, of how I deserve the best life ever.

I am relaxed and happy. I am relaxed and happy. I am relaxed and happy.

Possibility follows me wherever I go. It's all around me, and my footsteps move in the right direction, always attracting my dreams and goals.

I am expanded. I am empowered. I am a creator.

Exercises

What are some ways you will create an environment that supports a prosperity mindset? Think about changes you can make to your home, office, and even your car.

Think about a way to dress or look that inspires your new abundant lifestyle. Write down your ideas, and start doing one of them, even if just for fun.

Do you hold any grudges, anger, or resentment? Releasing your demons frees your heart, mind, and soul to move forward toward your dreams, instead of ruminating on the past. Write down anything that you'd like to drop and leave behind you permanently.

CHAPTER 13

FINDING YOUR MONEY ENERGY

The universe is abundant with everything you desire. It's not testing your ability to earn money; it's testing your ability to receive it. Align your thoughts and beliefs with abundance, and watch the flow of prosperity unfold.

— ESTHER HICKS

I know how to get myself into the right vibe for attracting abundance, and it is never from grasping tightly onto things. It is never clinging. It is never from a sense of lack or fear. Or not enough. It's the opposite. When I am relaxed and totally chilled out, as well as grateful and happy, celebrating my life, *those* are the times that I attract the most prosperity. Those are the times I am most creative, most focused, and most productive.

I use the word "attract" a lot because it has a magical feel to me. But it's not like I'm Luke Skywalker, pointing my finger, and the fat stack of Benjamins comes floating through the front door to me. (Though it's a fun mind picture.)

I know that when I have elevated emotions and incredible pictures in my mind, I have a boosted self-esteem and confidence, which, in turn, causes me to try new things and take more exciting chances. Or to bring the right people into my life at the right time. Or to come up with more ideas and create new projects.

When you're more relaxed, your brain's blood flow increases, allowing you to be more creative. It also increases your focus, which is important, because whatever you focus your attention on will grow, and you'll see more of it in your life.

Thinking and Feeling for Money

Neuroscientist Dr. Joe Dispenza teaches this idea that, when you want something in life, you should aim to be wanting it from an emotional position of power, of fulfillment. Not one of scarcity or lack, because these fear-based emotions get in the way and sabotage your progress. Therefore, part of the equation of attracting more abundance and prosperity into your life is to do it from the perspective of already having it.

Whaaaat?

If you want abundance in your life, you need to feel abundant now, no matter what your circumstances are. You have to feel abundance and prosperity now, where you are today, in order to attract and notice the opportunities that are all around you to help you reach your goals.

You can't walk through life expecting wealth while having a sour, fearful attitude. You'll only see crappy things. If you're focused on debt and lack, then that is what will stand out on the horizon. You'll see it everywhere you look... in the news, the economy, movements in the stock market, or things your friends or coworkers say about their own financial stresses. When fear controls your focus, these all become way too easy to latch onto. As opposed to focusing on solutions when you're primed for positive, constructive thinking.

I understand that sometimes it's hard for people to feel abundance, now, when they're buried under debt, or when they have a job where they can't imagine making the kind of money they would love to make. But that's where Money Self-Talk is the key! When you do your Money Self-Talk regularly, you start to feel it, and then you start to believe it, despite your circumstances. And when you start to believe it, that's when you're in the best possible position to make a change.

When I talk about having a positive energy and an incredibly high vibe, it only happens when you feel it deep within. So you need to really take a good look at your life and get rid of any part that brings your energy down. This might take some time... I speak from experience. The first step is being aware. Aware of your thoughts and your reactions to external things. And every time something happens that disrupts your positive vibe, ask yourself, *Could I respond better next time?*

I know someone who believes that "bad things always happen" to her. And this same person looks at me awestruck that everything just always seems to go my way. As though I've got some magic trick that makes everything work out. Well, I do! My self-talk! If you look closer at this person's life, you'll see that it is filled with judgment and constantly feeling negative. It's no wonder that's what she gets as a result!

It's time for you to rise up and become a new person. A person full of kindness, and generosity, and love, and excitement. A person who, when something negative happens, you instinctually look for the silver lining. The person people like to be around because it feels good to be around you. You're not just paying lip service to some vague notion of "positive thinking." No, you're committed. *All in.* This is a *lifestyle*. It's a way of life. A way to live. So take stock of your attitude, and choose to go big and be bold. So, even if the fire's at your feet, it doesn't matter... you hold your head high, and you know you'll thrive.

Abundance comes in all kinds of forms, not just money. So, to get a good sense of the broader meaning of "abundance," you want to look at every part of your life, to see where you can find it. Abundance can be having twenty cans of soup in your pantry. It can be a full cup of coffee, and when you look at it, steaming in front of you with the java scent wafting up your nose, take a moment and enjoy the abundance of the experience. It can be an abundance of sunshine. It can be an abundance of rain. It can be an abundance of having a full tank of gas. Or the love from your family. Or snuggles from your cat. Or kisses from your dog.

So if you ever feel like you're not living a life of abundance, it really helps to flip the script and list all of the things that are truly abundant in your life.

ZOOM OUT: That's the goal, you want to *feel* abundance in order to *attract* abundance.

Money Self-Talk Script

I feel abundance everywhere I look.

My life overflows with time, prosperity, and abundance.

I love manifesting and making my dreams come true.

I am full of loving energy, and I see abundance everywhere I turn.

I am full of abundance. My life is full of abundance.

When I fall asleep at night, I have an abundance of peace that my dreams are coming to me.

When I wake up in the morning, I exude smiles in abundance to start my day off just right.

Abundance is my natural state of being, and I attract it so easily.

I trust that prosperity and wealth are on their way to me.

I am open and receptive to all of the shimmering abundance that is coming straight to me.

I get to choose what to focus my mind on. My attention is my superpower.

I am surrounded by magnitudes of abundance. It's all around, WOW!

Prosperity flows into my life easily, and my arms are wide open for it.

My thoughts, feelings, and beliefs about abundance create my new reality, and I am ready for the most abundant life.

I am grateful for the abundance that exists within me and all through me. I allow it to radiate out into the beautiful world.

Exercise

You want to develop the habit of identifying things you have in abundance right here and right now. What are some things you have in abundance today?

CHAPTER 14

STRUCTURING YOUR DAY
FOR SUCCESS

To be rich in money, first one needs to be rich in productive habits.

— Anonymous

Behind any truly successful person, you'll find excellent habits.

Habits are actions you do routinely. They're so routine that you usually don't even think about them... you just do them. And they can change your life, because they can further your success by structuring your day better. They make it easier to stay focused and on track.

Although my day can be very flexible, when it has a backbone as its structure, it makes for sliding into my tasks much easier. I don't wake up and ask any questions about what to do... I just know. This creates a relaxed frame of mind and increased energy, as I don't waste any effort or suffer from decision-making fatigue. When I wake up, I always know what I'm going to do: Coffee/Money Self-Talk, morning walk, write, email. These habits ensure that my money train keeps rolling.

Take Note

You know how some people keep a food journal to track their calories and inspire better food choices? Well, I want you to keep a notebook and jot down *everything* you do—not just food-related—every day, for at least a few days. Perhaps at 6am you wake up, drink coffee, get the kids ready for school, and shower. At 7am, you go to work. What else do you do? How many minutes a day do you scroll through social media? Do you go to the drive-through for dinner or do you make dinner. Do you get back on social media again when you're home, or do you turn on the TV and veg out? Do you read? Do you exercise? Do you play video games? Go for a walk?

When you look back at your schedule, you might discover pockets of time, big or small, where you could work on new habits to help you get closer to your money dreams. For example, if you have a commute in the car, and you spend it listening to music or the radio, perhaps listen to an audiobook or a podcast to learn something new, and make it your new habit.

Persistence to Prosperity

Habits form over time. But you have to show up and do the behavior every day for a few weeks, and these will take root and become permanent, just like your self-talk becomes a belief when you say it every day for a while. Whether you want to exercise every day, or add the habit of reading one book a week, persistence is what makes it stick long term.

Scheduling Smartly

Once you've logged your behavior for a few days and taken a closer look for any patterns in your schedule, set yourself up for success by scheduling certain things *at certain times*, like when you're at your best physically or have the most mental energy. For example, I've learned that I'm most creative in the mornings and in the evenings, so I save the middle of the day for working out or tending to things that require less brain power. But going to the gym at night? No way. Everyone's different, however. For years, my husband worked out at 2am, and he loved having the gym all to himself.

Think about and write down any new habits you want to acquire, or new skills you want to learn. Then, find time in your day to do them regularly. You might consider going to bed earlier and waking earlier, to take advantage of pockets of energy or creativity, to work on making money. This might seem obvious, but you'd be amazed how many people don't have a consistent, thoughtfully devised schedule, with good habits and routines. Time just always seems to get away from them, and they never really make much consistent progress toward their goals.

Money Self-Talk Script

I am super smart with my time and my schedule. I optimize to magnetize and capitalize!

My mornings start with a bang, and I do my Money Self-Talk every day.

With the right schedule, I set up my day to be proactive with my success. Look at me go!

My brain is phenomenal, and I support it with great sleeping habits.

My body is strong, and I take care of it every day. It gives me the energy to power through.

I am filled with ideas, and I structure my day to take advantage of this power. I'm smart and creative with my time!

I am defined by the vision of living my richest life.

It's time to own my life. Right here. Right now. Watch me go.

What I appreciate, appreciates! I appreciate health, love, and success!

I'm living an extraordinary life, and I'm proud of how I'm building my desired outcome.

My life is expanding because of my courage to go after my dreams. Each upgrade I make to my life is practice for the next big step, and my self-talk is the key.

Oh my gosh! I did it! Everything I want is happening! Woohoo!

I feel wealthy today, because I know my dreams are coming true.

My job is knowing how worthy I am, how amazing my life is, and how powerful my mind is.

I have excellent habits, and I'm proud of them. I love taking care of myself, and it shows.

Exercise

Write down one to three new habits you want to acquire.

Now work out a schedule to start implementing them into your life, and add this schedule to your calendar.

CHAPTER 15

YOUR MONEY PEOPLE

The free soul is rare, but you know it when you see it—basically because you feel good, very good, when you are near or with them.

— CHARLES BUKOWSKI

When it comes to making more money, you may need to take a long, hard look at the people in your life. You've probably heard the expression, *We're most like the five people we spend the most time with.* Take note, and take heart. It's largely true. The people we spend the most time with tend to rub off on us.

Are you spending time with people who uplift you? Do they fill your cup with optimism? Are you spending time with people who elevate your emotions and inspire your money goals? Or are you with a bunch of peeps who drag you down, preventing your ship from sailing to brighter shores?

When you seek prosperity, you want to surround yourself with people who support that shimmering goal. When you're dreaming up new ways to make money, whether it's starting a new business, or learning new skills, or investing, or just being somebody who has an incredible mindset about attracting what you want... the people you spend the most time with will have an impact on your bottom line.

Proximity Power

How do you find supportive prosperity-minded people? Your *money tribe*? Begin by taking into account your *proximity* to prosperous and uplifting people (and environments). Discover where you can position yourself so opportunities easily find you. Get out there and show the universe you're ready to play ball. Go to where the magic is happening, like attending events, lectures, meeting people for coffee, or forming a mastermind group.

When I was a teen, my mom would drive me 45 minutes to the University of Michigan library just so I could study amongst all the cool college students. She hoped I'd be inspired by being around them, and it worked. A few years later, when it came time to start thinking about college, there was no doubt in my mind that I'd be going. And what school was my first choice? U-M, of course! *Go Blue!*

You can do the same kind of thing for your grown-up self, even if it means driving half an hour to plant your butt in a cafe on the ritzy side of town.

In other words... go to where the people with money are.

Ask Questions and Give Sincere Compliments

A great way to meet new people is to simply ask them questions and make small talk, like while waiting in line at the grocery store. Make small talk with people every chance you get. You can start by asking the butcher which product of theirs is their favorite, or ask someone in line at a café what they're going to get to drink, or if they've tried a particular item that you're considering. Compliment someone on their shirt, tie, shoes, or hair. You'll be amazed at some of the conversations you can have, and the things you can learn, just by putting yourself out there and asking an easy question.

You'll also be amazed at how giving small, genuine compliments can help you get out of sticky situations. We once had a challenge come up while working on our dual citizenship in Italy. The episode came to be known as the "Comma Drama."

Here's what happened... through my Italian ancestry, my daughter and I were eligible to obtain dual Italian/US citizenship and Italian passports, which would come in handy, as we were planning on living in Italy. However, in order to get an Italian passport, you first need a *carta d'identita,* which is your basic ID card. Getting mine was a breeze. Getting my daughter's, however, was not.

As we stood there, patiently waiting for the lady to enter my daughter's data into the computer, she started to get frustrated. Then, the *hand gestures* started as she used them to yell at her computer screen. Uh-oh, something wasn't right. Apparently, one of my daughter's documents had a comma between her first and middle name, and the others did *not* have a comma between her first and middle name. Italy wants these to match!

Who would've guessed that something as trivial as a comma could create such a headache? Well, the computer system did not like the comma, and it was going to require extra work to get this fixed—going outside of the normal process—in the already slow and bewilderingly complex Italian government bureaucracy. Our woman eventually escalated our problem to her superior, who soon escalated it to her boss, a distinguished looking older woman with green eye shadow. She seemed mildly bothered by all the fuss, and poised to rattle off the verdict, *"non é possibile"* (it's not possible).

I looked at her, and I found that I admired her green eye makeup, which was all the rage in Italy at the time. I quickly grabbed my phone and pulled up Google Translate.

"*Mi piace il tuo trucco,*" (I love your makeup). I pointed to my eye so she'd know I was referring to her eye shadow.

Well, hell's bells, you'd think I uttered a magic charm spell. *Her whole face lit up!* I think she was touched, knowing I didn't speak much Italian, but I had taken the time to compliment something so specific about her. Her whole vibe changed, and she seemed determined to do whatever it would take to fix our problem. And guess what? She ended up escalating our case from our little town's office all the way to Rome! (To the *Ministry of Punctuation,* probably.) Soon after, my daughter received her passport!

Mastermind Group

Mastermind groups have been around for a long time. Napoleon Hill coined the term in 1937 in his classic self-help book, *Think and Grow Rich.* Hill details the importance of finding your own mastermind group, which is basically a peer-to-peer mentoring group. Now, this isn't a social club, or a gossip group, or a place to complain about your ex. The group is designed to give advice, get advice, and to be motivated by like-minded people regarding everyone's goals.

Think about the people in your life, and consider forming your own mastermind group, even if it's just with one other person. The other person doesn't have to be doing the same thing as you. So long as you're both motivated and working on goals, you can help each other with ideas, solving problems, and staying focused.

I'm in a writer's mastermind group with a couple of badass author babes. We meet on Zoom every couple of weeks to talk about our current projects and to cheer each other on. We share ideas about marketing, writing, starting new projects, and we support each other with brainstorming and problem-solving. It also helps with creativity and firing up everyone's spirit. It's awesome.

Downer Peeps

Let's talk about the not-so-good people in life. This is an important topic, because, for as much as the good people lift you up, the not-so-good ones can drag you down. Those are the people you want to tell, *"Buh-bye."*

And guess what? You have permission to cut negative people out of your life, because you have the right to live your most amazing life. You have the right to run like hell from people who don't understand what you're doing. You have permission to end relationships that don't support your elevated mindset, *so you can make room* for the people who will shake their pompoms for you and cheer you on to the finish line. These people absolutely exist!

I find this process of letting go easier than some people do. But here's my bottom line: I'm unavailable for anything or anyone who's directly or indirectly trying to dull my shimmer and sparkle. I'm unavailable for negativity. And that's because I'm on a mission: to live my most magical life. I have big, brash, and outlandish ideas when it comes to money and my intimate relationship with it. I don't give a hoot if anybody thinks I'm nutty. And I refuse to drink another person's poison cocktail, even if it's offered with love. (And you know those people... they mean well.) And what if they're family? Well, I'll still see them at Thanksgiving, but I might be sitting at the other end of the dinner table!

It's actually really easy for me. Here's my simple formula: I pay attention to how I feel when I'm around someone, and I pay attention to how I feel when we part. If I feel worse when we're together, I inject some space between us and spend less time with that person. Sometimes this just means seeing them less often. In extreme cases, it might mean flat-out ending our relationship.

I have a family member who I'm sure has good intentions, but it seemed that he used to enjoy pushing my buttons with his snarky questions and comments. But he's family, and I love the stinker. So I'd just smile and keep going on my merry money-making way, but there are certain topics I won't discuss with him. Interesting thing though... over time, he has dialed down the snark, and now he's getting into this golden mindset stuff himself! I'm glad I didn't write him off; you never know when someone is going to get the manifesting bug, especially if your happiness is so contagious.

Sheep in Wolf's Clothing

All that said, there can be benefits to hanging around people who think differently. You can find gold nuggets of inspiration with people who hold opposing ideas. So I'm not suggesting you cut people out because they have different beliefs. But it's one thing to have a different perspective on the economy or politics, and quite another thing to be sinister or demeaning, with conversation that isn't uplifting, or at least educational.

Trust me, you'll know the difference! Put your hand over your heart and think about how you feel when you're with that person. If you feel challenged in a good way, then that's a source of inspiration. Keep them around! But if you feel dark, or defensive, or belittled, or just slimy after being around them, then perhaps that person is not a good influence. Good riddance!

Money Self-Talk Script

Everyone in my life wants the best for me, and I attract people like this.

My friends are supportive of my financial dreams!

I am surrounded by the coolest peeps, and we love making money! We are all fabulous. And all is fabulously well.

When I connect with like-minded souls, it's another way to get closer to my goals.

I rejoice, dance, and appreciate the success of others. This helps me grow and inspires me.

I love to meet new people. I'm always excited about where it might lead me.

Networking is a piece of cake, and I make it happen!

I give myself permission to end relationships with negative people.

I am ready for amazing friends, mentors, and teams. I am ready to inspire others with my vibe, and to absorb their positive vibes, too. We are all one.

I love my friends, and my friends love me. We are living our dream lives. Woohoo!

My inner circle is special and magical. I appreciate the different points of view we bring to the table.

When I connect with like-minded souls, it's another way to get closer to my goals.

I am worthy of meaningful relationships. I am worthy of love, and kindness, and support coming my way.

I love that so many people can depend on me, and that I have so many wonderful people I can depend on, too.

I love supporting my friends and loved ones. We love sharing great ideas together.

Exercises

Make a list of five places you can spend some time that increases your proximity to successful people. Make a plan to be at one, and put it on your calendar.

Make a list of successful people you know who will inspire your prosperity adventure. How can you spend more time with them? Can you form a group where you inspire each other?

Think about any people who are currently a negative influence in your life. What are some things you can do to decrease the effect they have on you?

CHAPTER 16

THE LEARNING LIFESTYLE

If you want to experience prosperity at a miraculous level, you must leave behind your old ways of thinking and develop a new way of imagining what is possible for you to experience in your life.

— WAYNE DYER

Think about it... you have the power to *reinvent* your financial self at any time. You have the right to go after wealth, prosperity, and joy. Most people would love to have more money, but the important question is, how much do you want it? Enough to do what it takes? Do you want to go after wealth like a little putt-putt golf cart, or like a Formula One race car?

I'm guessing the race car.

If so, we need to talk about the *Learning Lifestyle*.

My husband and I have long been fans of learning: acquiring new skills, reading, exploring new places, etc. We like the process of learning, and we love the *feeling* of our brains stretching and strengthening. In fact, we start to feel stagnant if just a few days go by without any learning. And the Learning Lifestyle makes our life *waaaaay* more fun and interesting.

Learning is how we thrive in the present.
And it's how we set ourselves up for success in the future.

Learning is how you stay relevant. It's how you stay marketable. And it's how you continuously improve your financial abundance. When does the learning stop? Never. That's why they call it *lifelong learning*.

Experts give the following success formula:

For every skill you acquire, you increase your odds of success.

What a great way to think about every new skill you learn or master. There's no doubt that learning can improve your life in many ways. You can accelerate your career, you can learn new skills for a whole new career, you can improve your resume, network with like-minded people... you might even meet someone in a class who changes your path in life!

When you think about living a lifestyle focused on never-ending learning, think *ka-ching!* And stick a dollar sign ($) on it, because you raise your market value when you learn new skills. And here's the amazing thing... you don't even have to be an expert or extraordinary at the thing you're learning. Just increasing your bag of tricks to a level of "good" can be ridiculously beneficial.

Here's a funny story... I once heard about a guy who taught himself how to do something called "pivot tables" in Microsoft Excel. He was no Excel power-user, just an average guy who sometimes did spread-sheets for his job. One day, just out of curiosity, he watched a couple of YouTube videos and learned how to do pivot tables in about an hour. He started using them for his job, and his non-Excel-savvy boss was *blown away*, like he'd invented quantum computers or some-thing, haha! Then they gave him a promotion to the job of "analyst"!

It gets even better though. In the guy's new role as an analyst, he kept adding to his Excel skills, little by little—again, with YouTube!—and he'd add things like macros and formulas to his spreadsheets, eventually creating something so useful that he'd generate charts for the executive team's weekly presentations. Now, he was the only person in the company who did this... he "owned" this particular business process. In doing so, he basically made himself *irreplaceable*. And a year later, when the company had layoffs, he was never at any risk of losing his job. Why? Because the higher ups needed their weekly charts. They had become dependent on him!

Stories abound of people using nothing more than YouTube videos to become professional photographers, 3D artists, software developers, and data scientists, or to pass a pharmacy licensing exam, or to save thousands of dollars by doing their own home and auto repairs. Many people have even used YouTube videos to learn how to build their own houses!

Like the saying says, *The more you learn, the more you earn.*

I think of learning as an essential nutrient to my bank account's health, and I prioritize learning by putting regular focus on it. Sometimes that means reading articles or books. Sometimes it's asking a friend questions about their job. Sometimes it's working on a new skill, like photography, or ping pong, or singing. Note that the skills aren't always obviously connected to making money... you often never know how things will pay off. But continuous learning eventually builds so much knowledge that you're simply more effective at life in general, no matter what you're working toward.

Take stock of your skills, and if you don't already have one, write down a list of new skills to learn, or current skills you'd like to improve. Doing this can not only increase your value in the workplace, but it also builds your confidence and self-esteem. As I write this, one of my best girlfriends is currently training to get her private pilot's license. How cool is that? It's a lifelong dream of hers, and besides a new ability—that she'll be able to *fly frickin' planes*—she's also benefiting from the learning process as she gains confidence, and it strengthens her brain. Such a bold thing will impact every part of her life, not only in ways she can imagine, but also in so many ways she can't yet.

Here are some ideas for *fundamental* skills that can improve your life:

- **Public speaking** – This is a powerful skill, and it's something you can learn. (Check out Toastmasters to get started.)

- **Comedy** – Humor is a super way to connect with people, and it makes networking much easier. People always love a funny person. To get started, take an improv class.

- **Speaking a foreign language** – This is a great skill, amazing for your brain's health, and you even learn things you never knew about your *own* language and culture. Check out the Duolingo app if you're just doing it for fun, and the Busuu app (or an online course) if you're more serious.

- **Advertising** – If you have a product to sell, then you'll probably want to learn about advertising and marketing. Check out Udemy.com for inexpensive classes to get you started.

- **Photography** – In today's day and age, with people sharing so many pictures online, I decided to take an inexpensive, online photography class. It only took me a couple of hours to go through, and I improved my photography skills instantly.

Learning Skills for Better Networking

There's another cool benefit to learning new skills: It can be a great form of networking. Whether it's taking a class and meeting like-minded folks, or it's giving you a new "thing" with which to connect to other people. For example, perhaps you learn how to sew clothes, and you share pictures of your creations on social media. This connects you to other people who share the same interest. You never know what might come of it... maybe a friend commissions you to make t-shirts for her children, and the kid wears them to school, where all the other little kids want one. Boom! New business venture! An acquaintance of my husband started a *million-dollar* baby clothing business doing exactly this.

The Most Successful People Are Out There... LEARNING!

The most successful people in the world live the Learning Lifestyle. Warren Buffett invests up to 80% of his time reading and thinking about his business. Bill Gates is known to take "reading vacations," where he goes on vacation and does nothing but read for a week. And Shark Tank billionaire Mark Cuban reads for 4 to 5 hours a day! As soon as he wakes up in the morning, he starts learning. And then there's Oprah Winfrey, who lives her life surrounded by books, and billionaire investor David Rubenstein, who tries to read 100 non-fiction books a year on a wide range of topics including business, history, and biographies of great people. These mega successful people are always reading, reading, reading, and always learning.

Do you read every day? If not, now is the time to start a new reading schedule. And if you say you don't have time, then you *don't have time to make more money.* Though you're reading this book now, so... *yay, you!*

Make time to read a little every day. Or a lot! You can listen to audiobooks in the car, on walks, at the gym, and while doing chores around the house. You'll probably learn more from reading non-fiction than fiction, but fiction is also important, especially for doing creative work and understanding people better.

A person who won't read has no advantage over one who can't read.

— MARK TWAIN

Daunting?

Does it feel overwhelming to add yet another priority to your life? I guarantee there are pockets in your day where you can find time to read or learn new skills. Even ten minutes a day is incredibly valuable, compared to nothing. Maybe it's something you do on the weekend. Or perhaps you wake up earlier each morning. Or cut out some TV, video games, or other leisure activity. Perhaps you take advantage of your commute time. Perhaps you dedicate entire vacations to reading or learning new skills! How fun—especially for a whole family! *Dude ranch, here I come!*

Money Self-Talk Script

I love learning new skills. I live the Learning Lifestyle, and this makes me more successful. It makes me more money!

Learning sparkly new skills is easy and fun for me.

I'm like a Swiss Army knife... I can do so many things.

When I learn new skills, I meet new people. It's awesome, and these connections create magical opportunities.

I love asking people questions, and I'm a great listener when people are talking.

I am ready to learn new skills. I am ready to love learning.

Reading enriches my life with cash and curiosity. I love reading every day!

My heart expands with strength and courage when I go after new skills. I revel in curiosity.

I am curious, tenacious, happy, and grateful to be alive.

Wonderful new opportunities to learn cool new skills are coming to me right now.

I read every day, because it's a smart thing to do. I love learning.

I deserve to have the prosperity I desire, and I'm excited about doing new things to make that happen.

I have arrived. I am successful. I have attracted and attained my incredible goals.

I encourage myself every day, because I can do it. I AM doing it.

I can choose to be great in any area that excites me. And I can certainly choose to be wealthy.

Exercises

Make a list of skills you want to acquire or things you want to learn more about.

CHAPTER 17

A DIFFERENT VIEW OF DEBT

Luck is what happens when preparation meets opportunity.

— SENECA

Debt and I go way back. I had a destructive relationship with it, and it destroyed my mood for years. I broke down and had fits. I cried and screamed. And I allowed this anxiety to fill me with the negative, survival emotions of fear and scarcity and lack. *Frankly, it suuuucked.*

But when I learned the power of the Magical Money Mindset, and I had a strategy for developing the mindset with Money Self-Talk, the debt ceased to be a noose around my neck. How did I do it? It started with changing my mindset about debt in particular. It sounds weird, but one of things I did was to view debt... more *positively*.

What? Come again?

How can debt be a good thing?

Let me explain. I decided to view all my past purchases that increased my debt as having served a beneficial purpose. For example, as a woman passionate about biohacking and longevity, my spending on supplements was beyond extravagant. Like, crazy even. I bought so many different herbs one time, that I had to buy an entire bookshelf just to hold them! My home became a mini apothecary, and from an herbal standpoint, we were ready for any zombie apocalypse.

And then there was the $2000 Norwalk juicer I bought on credit. Of course, I always had a solid rationale for big purchases like these. This was the Cadillac of juicers, *but it squeezed 20% more juice out of veggies than $200 juicers, so eventually I'd break even from buying less produce, right? I mean, it's just math.*

Technically, this was true... but it would take me *ten years*!

And then there were legit expenditures, actual necessities, like that trip to the emergency room. Or the puppy I found abandoned in the desert with a broken leg. What was I supposed to do, leave him there? Well, $3000 on my credit card later, he was fine, with his little green cast and needing a home. I didn't regret paying his vet bill for one moment.

And there were our fertility expenses. We spent almost fifty thousand dollars to get pregnant. Do I regret that? Obviously not. We now have a daughter.

So yeah, I racked up a lot of debt, and I had good reasons for a lot of it. Maybe some of the things I could've gone without. But should I have broken down every month when the credit card bill came and destroyed my good vibes? No. It never helped me to scream or complain about it. It would have just made me feel crappy and guilty. I needed a different way to see my debt to improve my outlook.

This emphasis on my outlook might seem trivial, but it was a big deal for me... one day I realized something interesting. That my mindset —*back when I made those purchases*—was one of excitement. And so, I very simply chose to see my past purchases as *having served me well*. Not as something to stress about now.

Could I have done without the fancy cold-pressed juicer? Yes, absolutely. But I sure jumped for joy buying that thing, and I have to think that, at some level, the purchase created positive energy every time I used the juicer, and every time I drank the delicious juice from it. So it wasn't *all* bad.

This new mindset allowed me to give my past self a hug for the extravagances. And most importantly, to *let go of the guilt*. This way, when the bills came, I didn't freak out and drop my vibe every time or punish myself for past missteps.

Don't get me wrong... I rarely spend money frivolously now, and I'm not suggesting that irresponsible spending is ok just because it makes you feel good. I'm saying that, once you correct the behavior, there's no benefit to beating up your past self about mistakes you've made. You've learned your lesson and you move on, a much wiser person.

Sometimes, it's these small shifts in mindset that make the difference between flying high or falling into a black hole of despair. And since we're all about maintaining that high vibe, I do everything I can to support that.

My Freaky Frugal Days

And then there was the time I went *super frugal* to pay off the debt...

Years before I changed my mindset with my Coffee Self-Talk ritual, I grabbed my debt by the throat and tried to squeeze it to death. As a person who can sometimes tend toward extremes (vegan diet, carnivore diet, selling everything to travel the world, etc.), it came as no surprise when, in my desperation, I suddenly went *extreeeeme* with frugality.

I did a complete budget overhaul, scrutinizing every penny we spent. We made good money, but not enough surplus to pay down significant debt. Since we didn't expect any big windfalls of cash to come in,

I figured I'd attack the debt from the other end, by cutting spending. *Drastically.*

I'm talkin' full-blown *austerity measures.*

I got out my trusty budget spreadsheet, and I started making radical changes. For instance, because we lived in Arizona, with its center-of-the-sun summer heat, I put our toaster oven out on the patio so it wouldn't heat up the kitchen. But then I went further... I kept the air conditioning set to 83°F. Even with fans, this made us all uncomfortable, and we turned into sloths. It's not easy to work when you're dripping sweat and your energy is sapped. But I didn't care. It saved a couple hundred bucks a month, and I was at war with my debt.

I calculated the cost per gram of protein for various foods, and we'd eat the cheapest protein (beans and sardines). I air dried our laundry. When my husband pointed out that the towels were "scratchy," I told him to think of it as "exfoliation." I became an expert at loading the dishwasher, so no space was left empty. I drove super slowly so I didn't waste gas. I could go on and on.

Did all of these extreme measures move the needle on my debt?

Only a little. What really mattered was stopping buying so much stuff I didn't need. And ironically, by traveling abroad, where we slashed our expenses by housesitting and not paying rent, utilities, car payment, gas, or outrageous U.S. healthcare premiums. (Funny thing, I did use what I learned from my frugality adventure in a romance novel I wrote, *Count on Me...* so there's that.)

I'm not sure which nightmares are worse for my husband, memories of the time I urged him to eat vegan, which meant no more delicious cheeseburgers, or the time I took us on the extreme frugal journey. God love him though, he's slept in the jungles of Guatemala and doesn't complain about much (except scratchy towels), and he always goes along with my wacky experiments.

Was Frugal Worth It?

Here's what I know… the feelings I had during that frugal time were of a very *low* vibration, and that was a big problem. That whole period of time felt like one long slog of lack and scarcity, which I think might have just attracted more of that to me, because it's all I saw. It was my complete, obsessive focus. My entire *worldview*. And although I had a few moments of joy when we paid down a small chunk of debt, it was a small moment compared to the lengthy period of pain from actually living in that deep, frugal state of mind. Spending an entire month sweating in your undies while blogging because the air conditioning isn't on, eating beans and rice, and feeling this constant low hum of *constraint*… compared to the one moment per month that I paid off a small chunk of debt…

I don't know. I'm not sure it was worth it.

That's not to say there isn't somebody out there who can go extremely frugal and love it. But it wasn't just me existing in my strange frugal reality, there was my husband and my daughter to consider. And let me tell you, my daughter did *not* love it, and that's putting it mildly. Not only did I say no to *everything*, but in hindsight, I recoil at the anguish and anxiety—and maybe even long-term damage to her own self-talk—when I'd say, day after day, *"WE CAN'T AFFORD THAT!"*

It was soul crushing for everyone around. It was a polluting, negative, smog-like vibe that constantly floated through our house.

> *The words you speak become the house you live in.*
>
> — HAFIZ

My frugal experiment never made much of a dent in our debt. My focus was so narrow, and I always felt the weight of debt behind every thought and decision. There was no sparkle or magic in our lives.

Worst of all, *there were no big ideas.*

And it would be the *big ideas* that ended up whisking away $100K of debt like it was nothing, and then propelling us into real wealth.

You just can't think big when you're focused exclusively on survival. Even if you're in a tough spot, you still need to find a way to carve out a space for thinking big, for thinking about the possibilities beyond your immediate circumstances. You do this, as I've said, by changing your mindset. And you change your mindset with Money Self-Talk.

Everything brightened when I changed my mindset about money, using the power of my self-talk. I still had the same amount of debt initially—so nothing about our finances had changed—but the *feeling inside me* was the exact opposite, like night and day!

I *chose* to see expansive possibilities and money all around me. *I chose to believe* we'd pay it off, even though I didn't know how. I chose to be *confident*. I chose a joyful mindset. I chose not to freak out about every penny, but rather, simply to be smart about the things we bought.

And *that's* when things changed for us financially. The debt didn't decrease overnight, but my new mindset started lining things up in my life that would pay it down fast. It got our creative juices flowing... there was a noticeable change in the things we'd talk about, the things we'd try, the plans we'd make. And once that ship turned, we had *fast success* with our efforts.

Love Yourself Anyway, and Love Your Debt

One of the reasons debt created so much anxiety in me was that I felt guilty about it. I felt like a bad mom and wife for having spent so much money. But one day, I was sitting on my couch and thinking about self-love, and I realized that, as long as I held onto that guilt, I was not loving myself. So I jumped off the couch and suddenly decided, *I loved myself anyway, bad money decisions and all!*

This was a pivotal moment for me. It was like washing the slate clean. That's how powerful words can be. I was so excited about this change that I took it a step further and bellowed, *"You know what? I even **love** my debt."*

Ha! How's that for wild? Loving my debt?

That's right.

Why did I decide to love my debt? Because *love heals.* Love makes magic happen. Naturally, it felt a bit bizarre to love my debt, and I didn't know if I was losing my mind, but *I liked the way it felt.*

Your perception of anything negative changes when you shoot arrows of love at it: debt, wrinkles, illness, mistakes... everything. When you love yourself—now and completely—regardless of your debt, challenges, imperfections, whatever, then you can more easily see what you desire and take steps toward that thing, whether it's health, love, success, or prosperity. Why? Because your vibration is drastically different. It's elevated. There's an expensiveness—*literally!*—in your chest when you feel love, and that feeling works miracles.

That feeling should be the measuring stick by which we live our lives.

Money Self-Talk Script

I am worthy of love, respect, and prosperity.

I am calm and wildly happy.

I have an incredible relationship with money. I have an incredible relationship with me.

I honor my past, and I learn from it.

I see my life filled with financial peace and harmony. It's incredible, and I deserve it. We all do.

I always figure out what needs to be done with ease, because I'm smart. I'm a rockstar when it comes to learning.

I am free and wide awake to make great decisions and to take control of my life. Starting now.

I focus on my wins, and there are tons. I focus on the power inside my own beautiful mind. It's there at all times.

I am confident. I am confident. I am roaring with confidence! ROAAARRRRRRR!!!!!

I am in awe and wonder with my mind and the power of belief. I know my success starts with my mind. Yes.

I am strong, healthy, powerful, and resilient. I am strong, healthy, powerful, and resilient.

I am happy to be alive. What an incredible ride!

I am transformed, and then I transform some more. Life is amazing. I am grateful and full of love.

My personality is radiant, uplifting, and dynamic. I am confident, kind, and courageous.

My magical song pulses inside me, beating like drums of shiny prosperity.

Exercise

If you carry a lot of debt, take some time to write down how you got there, how it served you, and how you're moving past it. Make sure you include lots of love and forgiveness, if you feel otherwise.

CHAPTER 18

MAGICAL MONEY MIND

Always think of what you have to do as easy, and it will become so.

— Émile Coué

I've always marched to the beat of my own drum. As a young girl, I loved dolls and ribbons, and hanging with the boys and playing army dodge. I was a girly tomboy. I wanted to play rough and do "boy" sports like skateboarding, but I wanted to do it in my pleated skirt and penny loafers while wearing long pigtails with blue-checkered bows.

Because, you know what?

I wasn't going to let anyone define me but me.

And here I am today... still doing things in my own way. My magical money mind is no exception.

One of the biggest mistakes people make is accepting life as normal or "right" just because everyone else is marching to *that* drummer. But when you step out of the mainstream and innovate your thinking, that's when real change happens. That's when the possibilities show up. You start to see doors of opportunity all around you. *These doors are always there... most people are just blind to them.*

So it's time to program yourself to have the Magical Money Mindset, where you think and feel about money in exponential ways, at all times!

If what I'm doing sounds reasonable to most people, then I'm not working in a space that is creative and innovative enough.

— JANE MCGONIGAL

Mind Your Words About Wealth

One day, I was scrolling through Instagram, and an ad came up for a fancy-shmancy $500 face cream. Wow... that's way more than most creams on the market, and it made me curious as to whether there had been a scientific breakthrough I hadn't heard about, like some kind of quantum nano mitochondrial unicorn horn dust.

So I started reading the comments to see if there were people who'd tried the cream and written about their experience. It only took about ten seconds before I was shaking my head and closing out of the ad.

Why?

Because the comments were useless. In fact, they were borderline harmful, and I didn't want myself exposed to that. What was harmful about them? Comment after comment was filled with people *complaining about the price* of the cream—not people talking about loving or hating it—in fact, they hadn't even tried it. They were saying things like, *"How can anybody afford that?"* Or, *"That's way too expensive!"* And on and on.

There was a time when I used the words "can't afford," but I permanently exorcised that language out of my brain when I realized how powerful my words are in creating my reality. That doesn't mean I buy every single thing I see, but I sure as heck don't have a mindset that tells me I can't afford something. And I certainly don't surround myself with people who believe that expensive things must be automatically bad. Some things are worth paying more for.

When I created new language for my money mindset, sure, there were still things that wouldn't have been prudent to purchase. But I didn't say about them, *"I can't afford it."* In fact, I told myself, *"I can totally afford that."* Then, I went about my day, not buying the thing.

Indeed, I don't buy *most* of the things I tell myself I can afford, but it's important that I maintain the *mentality* that I *can* afford it. This is the opposite of having a scarcity mindset that holds you back.

This is a great lesson. People often look at something and think about whether they *can* or *can't* afford it. Language is king, and strengthening your words, and therefore your brain, is the first step to changing your finances, whether it's about affording $500 face cream or a mansion with ten acres. And it's not lying to yourself... this isn't about deception, it's about reprogramming your brain with specific language about the future you're creating.

So make manifesting wealth easier on yourself. Don't make it an uphill grind with poor language choices. Stop thinking about all the reasons you can't do something, or afford something, and instead think about all the reasons you can. Starting with the fact that you're worthy, you're wonderful, you're resourceful, you're kind, you're smart, and you're mega amazing.

Choose powerful words, and you will have a powerful life. Be confident about your prosperity, and constantly remind yourself that you have the *special sauce* to make your money dreams come true.

No one ever got rich by studying poverty and thinking about poverty.

— WALLACE D. WATTLES

Think About What You Want... NOT What You Don't Want

A big lesson in having the Magical Money Mindset is filling your head with pictures about the things *you want*. That means you must get rid of any pictures of things you *don't want*.

There was a time we were living in a rather shitty temporary apartment in Italy. But I had a choice for how I viewed my surroundings, including the impossible-to-clean sticky oil coating the walls by the stove (from previous tenants), or the sewage smell outside the bathroom window. Sure, I could look around the apartment and see all the things I didn't like. I could have whined and moaned about it.

But when you focus on things you *don't like*, there's a sneaky thing that happens: Your vibe takes a nosedive, and you notice these things even more.

Seeing more of negative things you already know exist does nothing to help you attract all the incredible things you want. When you're running away from the darkness, you want your mindset to be focused on running toward the light. Why? Because fear takes a toll. Yes, fear can be motivating, but being driven by fear comes at a huge price to your mind, body, and soul.

So, instead of thinking about the things I didn't like about the apartment, I shut the door on those thoughts and opened a new door. I walked into a room in my mind where I imagined my perfect apartment. I thought about all the things I *did* want. I thought of my dream place filled with fresh air, lots of windows, quiet, non-smoking neighbors, and awesome, sparkly kitchen appliances that weren't coated in grimy slop.

And what happened when I refocused my thoughts? I *instantly* lifted my energy.

This is so important!

But to make this your default way of thinking, you must train your brain. Instead, most of us fall prey to complaining about things we don't like. But bitching is 100% counterproductive. When we bitch, we radiate the wrong vibration. Thereby causing us to only see things we don't want, which makes us feel moody about other aspects of our life. It can even make us feel cursed, or like a failure.

New Life Rule!

Instead of saying what you don't like, say *what you **do** like*. Always.

When I witnessed the power of this language switch about my slimy apartment, I realized I should change my words about my debt, too. I didn't think about *not wanting* debt. Instead, I focused on what I *did* want, such as all the things I wanted to do and buy, and all the money I knew would be coming into my life somehow. In this way, I leapfrogged the debt topic by filling my mind with things I planned on buying once the debt was paid off: a new car, new house, first-class travel, etc.

Can you see how powerful this switcharoo is for your brain and mindset?

This doesn't mean you never think about things you don't like. Sometimes, noting the things we don't like is what helps us figure out what we want. The point is to not *stew* in the *don't likes*. Don't be consumed by them. Don't be a complainer. Don't whine. Instead, you want to shine, and this will get you to what you want faster, and you'll enjoy the process more.

The Abundance of Sardines

Let's talk about the importance of feeling abundant *right now*, no matter what your current financial circumstances are. In other words, *feeling* abundance before you *have* abundance.

What you appreciate, appreciates. The feeling of prosperity produces more prosperity. But I know what you're thinking. *How do you feel abundant if you don't actually have abundance?* Well, there's a hack to tapping into that, and you can do it right now.

I did it with sardines.

Sardines?

Yes, that happens to be my personal example, but you can apply it to anything you like.

You see, as I mentioned before, sardines are a fairly inexpensive source of protein. So, at any given time, my cabinet will have *dozens* of cans of sardines—*an abundance of sardines,* if you will. (Are you scoffing? I know, not everyone likes sardines, but hear me out.)

I look at things in my life that are *actually* in abundance. Things I have plenty of, or more than enough. I look around the house and ask, have I got enough of those? I usually do. Do I have enough dish towels? Yep, don't need any more, wouldn't buy any even if I were a billionaire. When it comes to dish towels, I'm Bill Gates' equal. We've both got enough. See how neat that works? *That's* how I tap into that abundant feeling, anytime I want.

I do the same thing with books when I'm at my mom's house. She has bookshelves that cover the walls, and when I stand amidst all those books, I feel abundance because there are so many books, so many ideas within those books, so many lessons to learn.

You can do this with anything in your life. Whether it's having an abundance of coffee in your house right now, or a full tank of gas in your car, or perhaps a closet full of clothes. Tap into that, and feel abundance from having an abundant amount *of something.* And use this feeling on a regular basis to then think about a future with an abundance of money. The feeling is similar. Abundance is everywhere when you look for it, even if you just start with sardines.

Remember:

To have more abundance,
*first create the **feeling** of abundance.*

From Happy Sexy Millionaire to Happy Sexy *Billionaire*?

If you've read *Coffee Self-Talk*, then you know there was a time I created an image in my mind of a "Happy Sexy Millionaire" to represent my goals. But one day, I was walking outside, the sun was shining bright, and my mindset got even more expansive. I thought, "What about Happy Sexy *Multi*-millionaire?"

And I stopped walking.

Hm. Interesting. Something was shifting inside me.

Then I said, "Wait a minute, what about Happy Sexy *Billionaire*?"

(Note: I probably don't actually seek to become a billionaire... seems like it might be more trouble than it's worth, and I value simplicity. Honestly, I'd much rather read a good book in a cabin than fly to Davos to mingle with world leaders. But run with me on this billionaire theme for a bit... it's fun. And if you seek to become a billionaire yourself, well I'm rootin' for ya!)

In that moment, I realized that, by upgrading from millionaire, to *multi*-millionaire, to *billionaire*, I created a totally different sensation inside me for each level. And each sensation created a different focus, filled with different ideas. At that time in my life, I was well on my way to reaching my current money goals, and I could easily come up with a straightforward plan for becoming a millionaire. I had many ideas for products and ways it could happen.

But wait! When I thought about what it would take to become a *multi*-millionaire, those thoughts and plans shifted a little. That was so interesting to me, but it made sense. To get different results, it requires doing different things.

And then, when I thought about becoming a Happy Sexy *Billionaire*, the plan shifted *a lot*, because the things it would take to become a billionaire versus a millionaire are very different.

Perhaps thousands of authors have become millionaires on book sales alone, or related spin-off opportunities, such as speaking, etc. But there's only one author who's made a billion dollars from books and spin-offs, JK Rowling. So if you wanted to join the *Three Comma Club*, you'd need a different strategy, such as starting a company, investing, inventing something ground-breaking, etc.

They might take a lot of time, effort, and some luck, but in principle, none of these paths are unattainable. I personally like thinking about billionaire-ness sometimes, not because that's my goal, but because it suddenly makes numbers like ten million seem eminently feasible, almost mundane. Like, how hard can it be, right? Haha.

A good way to start thinking big is imagining your target net worth goal, and then double or 5x that number... or 10x if you're feeling extra ambitious. Think about what it would take to make that much money, and what you could do with it.

Notice the shift that comes over you as you seriously contemplate the larger number. Then take advantage of this shift to come up with new ideas for making money.

When you think exponentially, it shakes up your brain because the idea is so big. It forces you to think outside your old mental frame. This big idea creates a big mindset, which can put you on a completely different path.

Even if you don't want to become a billionaire, merely imagining it might give you one great idea that's bigger than anything you would've thought of if you were just thinking about making a million, or some lower number, like $100,000.

Let your mind wander deep into Wild West territory... you never know where you'll strike gold.

Money Self-Talk Script

I have new ideas every day for generating wealth and streams of income.

Money and opportunities flow to me freely as I move through my world, as I step through my day. They're everywhere.

I love experimenting and trying new things, because it increases my creativity, which then helps me make more money!

I just have fun, and the money comes. Woohoo!

My big thoughts lead to big ideas, which lead to big success.

My spending is perfect. When I release money, more comes back to me. I know this, because my energy and mindset make my dreams come true. It's all up to me.

Mountains, oceans, and first-class luxury... that's my destiny. I am worthy of it all. We all are.

More money is always coming into my bank account.

I am a kind and generous person, and money expands every part of my life.

My income is constantly increasing. Money is overflowing in my life.

I am in charge. I am the creator. I am the master conductor.

I'm like iron... strong and forged in my own fiery mind, heart, and soul. I make it happen.

My intuition is like a GPS for my super-powered soul, and it knows the best routes to take. I pay attention to it. I see the signs. I follow them. I honor them. My intuition is incredible.

I am grateful for everything I have. I am grateful for being able to live my dream life.

Making money is in my blood. Yeah, baby!

Exercises

It's time to realign your thoughts. Take a minute to imagine being a millionaire, and then take a minute to imagine being a multi-million-aire. And then, just for fun, take a minute to visualize being a *billion-aire.* Even if this isn't your goal, visualizing the big version of something makes the smaller version seem much easier to your brain. Besides, *it's fun, right?* Write down what your new life is like.

_____

_____

_____

_____

_____

_____

_____

Too often, we default to thinking about things we don't like, or that focus our attention on the wrong things. To reprogram our brains with the Magical Money Mindset, we need to regularly change that. Sticky notes are a great reminder for this. On a few sticky notes, write reminders to keep your mindset focused on your goals and things you like, rather than on distractions and things you don't like. Stick them places where you'll see them throughout the day, such as on mirrors, the dashboard of your car, your refrigerator, your desk, etc.

CHAPTER 19

CASHIN' IN WITH CONFIDENCE

The greatest discovery of my generation is that human beings can alter their lives by altering their attitudes of mind.

— WILLIAM JAMES

I used to have zero confidence in my storytelling abilities. Scratch that—*I had negative confidence.*

I mean, for heaven's sake, I couldn't even come up with stories for my daughter when she was four years old. When it came time to play dolls, I pushed my husband into her bedroom to do it. And, man-oh-man, *he was good.* He grabbed those dolls with gusto, a story building in his eyes, and the two of them sat on the floor, diving into the most legendary scenarios. They'd have the dolls start companies, with all-female executive teams, corporate mergers, and there'd be hiring and firing, inventions, an epic dogfood and electric car factory made of Lego, and of course... ninjas.

Greg was a master at inventing excellent stories on the fly, and I used to stand from the doorway, mouth hitting the floor, in awe. *How does he just make shit up like that?*

Then I'd close my mouth and remind myself that he was a creator, naturally. That's how he did it.

And I was not.

What a crappy thing to tell myself, right? This was before I knew the power of self-talk.

Fast forward a few years. I was doing my Coffee Self-Talk every day, and I had a general script I used about abundance, health, parenting, romance, and magical living in general—all wrapped into one. But at the time, I had no idea what to do to bring in more money. So one day, I added a few lines to that all-purpose self-talk script about writing and storytelling. My Coffee Self-Talk ritual was already making sweeping changes in my life, with stress, self-esteem, and my anxiety, so I thought, *What the hell, it can't hurt. Who knows what might come of it.*

The lines were the following:

> *I am a creative genius.*
> *I am a prolific writer.*
> *I am filled with stories.*

I didn't do anything new, other than reading my script with these new lines snuck in. In time, it changed my life. If you've read *Coffee Self-Talk,* you know what happened...

One day, months after I'd added those lines, the pandemic lockdown had just begun, and I was sitting in my mom's backyard. Suddenly, out of the blue, guess what happened? I had a story idea for a romance novel, my first ever.

Yeah, me! And I ran with it, fleshing out every detail of the story, like I was channeling it from the ether. It was *effortless.* I was so exhilarated. It felt amazing!

Fast forward to today, and I now have ten romance novels under my belt. Remember, this is the lady who couldn't make up a doll story to save her life.

Here's a fun update since publishing *Coffee Self-Talk*. I had also written an entire self-talk script for author success, and one of the lines in that script stated that my work would reach an *Amazon Best Seller's Rank* of 107 or less. Meaning my book was in the top 107 books selling on all of Amazon, with the lower the number the better. Why 107? Just to have a weird number in my mind to make it stand out. Well, guess what? As of this writing, one of my books hit #32 in the entire Amazon store.

This is an epic example of transformation: I had started out with *zero* confidence about storytelling.

But I flipped the script. I changed the story in my head about my abilities, and my life's story changed as a result. *You can do this, too.* You can learn how to do something that you might not think you're capable of doing, because you're going to use your self-talk to change the story you tell yourself about that ability.

From Story Idea to Actual Writing

When I realized I had a romance story to tell, I didn't just automatically know how to write it as a book. I mean, that's a whole other skill set than just coming up with the ideas. But I did have the *confidence* that I could figure out the process, that it was a *learnable skill*. So I started reading and researching everything I could get my hands on about how to write novels.

And what else did I do? I kept on using my self-talk, of course! I used it to boost my confidence for going after this new goal of learning the writing process. I wrote specific lines about boosting my confidence and skills in writing, learning, and marketing these novels. I wrote affirmations about how *"I write great dialogue,"* and *"I write sizzling scenes."*

Many people don't realize they can use positive self-talk for *everything*. And I didn't let fears of how my novels would be received deter me, either. I didn't let lack of confidence deter me. I didn't think to myself, *"But, but, but... I didn't go to school to be a writer! I've never written a line of dialogue in my life!"*

Because, *who cares?*

When I released my books into the world, I did it with spunk and a smile. I boldly declared, *"Here you go, world! Here's my art!"*

I put my ass in the arena. Because you know what? That's the difference between people who do nothing and people who go for it. That's the difference between the strong and the weak. Most people are too scared of failure or embarrassment to go after what they want. But not me. I've got self-talk. I knock those fears to the curb, and you can, too. You can use your self-talk to get there.

You Have Permission to Not Give a Hoot

At any given time, others might say something I'm doing is either risky or crazy, or they might not believe my goals are attainable. But I don't mind. Like when I blogged that I'd be a millionaire while I was still buried in debt. I mentioned this to a friend, and she gave me a patronizing smile with a slight, disbelieving look.

I thought, *She doesn't get it. That's all right. What matters is that I'm going for it.*

Because here's the thing:

> *You have permission to not let what's happening outside of you
> mess with your dreams, goals, self-talk, and actions.*

I don't care what the circumstances are in the world outside you, or what people say... you have permission to not give a hoot about it. That includes family, friends, people on social media, random strangers' opinions, and anybody's *woe is me* stories of pessimism and learned helplessness.

Just because *they* can't do something doesn't mean *you* can't.

When I started writing romance novels, the pandemic was just hitting the U.S. It was all over the news, 24/7, and it was the only thing anybody was talking about. The whole world was either glued to the TV news or constantly hitting refresh on their Web browsers for updates.

Well, I did *not* get sucked into that. No sir. What did I do? I sat my ass down, and I wrote, wrote, wrote. I did not obsessively check the news, and I didn't talk to anyone else about it. The result? My mental well-being *thrived* during that dark time, when the world was freaking out.

Because I gave myself *permission* not to let the pandemic impact me.

I don't mean that we didn't take precautions, wear masks, stay at home, etc. By "not impacting me," I mean that it didn't affect my spirit. My mood. My thoughts. My creative work. These were all virtually unchanged, or even enhanced, as lockdown eliminated a lot of distractions as the outside world somewhat faded from view.

Remember how lots of people started baking bread for something to do during the pandemic? Well, I literally stayed home and wrote novels for a year. Honestly, I loved every minute of it.

Now, I'm well aware that our privileged, work-from-home status made our experience during that time much easier than most people had it, to say nothing of the tragic illnesses and deaths. I'm talking about the massive *psychological* toll the experience had on people. The depression. The anxiety. The sense of helplessness. Even for people who had things pretty easy like me, many of them didn't fare well psychologically.

What was the difference between my experience and theirs?

I kept my self-talk *extra* potent and powerful. I turned off the news, which kept talking and talking even when they had nothing new to say. I didn't need them filling the silence, and the world didn't need me stressing about things and adding to the collective freak-out vibe.

No! The world needed more uplifted energy. So I did my part, stayed positive, hopeful, and I shared that with friends and loved ones. I kept busy and focused on making my life amazing, learning, leveling up, and braving new things like writing my novels.

Because what you think about is a *choice*.

You don't have to jump on the bandwagon with everybody else when it comes to click bait, sad stories, or drama. The last time someone in my family shared "sad" gossip with me about something her friend texted her, I politely said, "Look, that's not the story I want playing in my head today. Let's talk about positive things instead."

This is one of the most important lessons I learned on this journey, because *there will always be something going on in the world*. It's just nature. But that doesn't mean you have to react like everyone else does. Close the door on things that are trying to steal your focus and distract you. The world will have shootings, and recessions, and deaths, and divisive politics, and wars, and illness, and pandemics. You do not have to let that knock you off track.

No, my friend, you can find your hundred percent, in every situation.

Does this seem cold-hearted? It's not at all. I care deeply about the world and other people. But I don't worry about things I can't change. Meanwhile, the thing that we *do* have control over is our thoughts and our actions. And with practice, our mood in general. You want to put positive energy into your life, and into the world, and in order to do this, *you must focus on good things*. During the pandemic, my mindset was thriving, not just surviving. My family benefited from this. My daughter benefited from this tremendously! I benefited from this. My home was *not* wrapped in fear. We had *fun*. This is a good thing!

And this doesn't mean you can't have wide-ranging conversations with people. My point in all this is to give you permission to decide what's best *for you*. You don't have to partake in other people's negativity. What you let into your mind, and how you process it, is a choice. You have control over your mind.

Four Tricks to Boost Your Confidence

Here are four fun tricks you can use to boost your confidence.

1. The "Of Course" Swagger Self-Talk

There's something about the expression "of course" that breeds epic confidence. It conveys a sense of sassy expectation. And expectation is a tantalizing flavor of belief. When I think about things I want in my life, like money, or land, or horses, or working from home, or donating to my favorite charities, I add those two simple words to the thought or affirmation:

Of course I can live in an amazing house
with land, and trees, and epic views.

Of course I can go back to school at age 45
and get a degree in anything I want.

Of course sales keep coming in every day, all day long.
I am wealthy, and money chases me down. *Of course!*

I am confident. I am wild. I am worthy of
everything I want. And I am fierce. *Of course!*

I am love. I am happiness.
I am success. *Of course!*

See how those two little words add swagger to your affirmations?

Language is powerful, so I take full advantage of it. When I add *of course* to an affirmation, it's like a big, glittery "duh!" And the reason it works is because—behind those two words—is a lightning bolt of *worthiness*. When you have that mindset that *of course* you can have something, that *of course* you deserve your heart's desires, and *of course* you can go after your goals, it means *of course... because you are worthy*. Of course!

2. Wear Your Sherlock Holmes Hat

As I've mentioned, language powers your goals and dreams, making them easier to realize. And just like language, *symbolism* is equally powerful.

When you have something in your life acting as a symbol, it does something special: It triggers a reminder. Sometimes we can get wrapped up in our day and become slightly unfocused, but when you have or do something *symbolic*, it reminds you to keep your butt on track.

What do I mean by *symbol*?

Your symbol could be anything. It could be something physical, like a beautiful piece of art. Or it could be a symbolic act, like taking a bath every evening, or making a point to watch the sun set.

But today, I'm talking about a specific symbol: putting on your "can-do" hat. Or, as I like to call it, my *Sherlock Holmes Hat*. I'm being quite literal: I have a white hat, bedazzled with pearly and glittery baubles, and when I wear it, I tell myself that *I can do anything*. And I have done this so many times that, as silly as it sounds, it works. You know, that train-your-brain stuff!

I have a rule about this hat: *I am particular when I wear it*. I throw it on anytime a challenge or roadblock comes up. For example, if I need to come up with a twist for one of my novels, I put on my hat. If I need to come up with a new product idea, I put on my hat. If I have a marketing challenge, I put on my hat.

When I put on my special hat, that's when I stop obsessing about roadblocks, and I change my thinking to open-mindedness, creativity, and problem-solving. Just like Sherlock Holmes solving mysteries, I solve my problems. My confidence ratchets up!

Do you have a special hat you can wear for solving problems? It shouldn't be a hat you wear at other times, so you might want to go get one! Or if you prefer, replace the hat with some other symbol. In Lemony Snicket's *A Series of Unfortunate Events* children's book and TV series, the character, Violet, ties her hair in a ribbon whenever she needs to tap into her genius problem-solving skills. Isn't that great? Whenever she ties up her hair, you know she's about to unleash some superpower. That's what you'll do, too, when you find your *problem-solving symbol*.

3. Know When to Be Eggy Versus Spermy

Have you ever seen a video of a microscope showing sperm zipping around? Those little buggers work hard and move as fast as they can toward the prize, the egg. Well, I use this bizarre metaphor to relax my efforts, sit back, and let money and customers *come to me*. In other words, I use this image to help me surrender. To help me be, well, more *eggy,* while all that busy-ness happens around me, and stuff comes to me *without me having to do anything.*

Being an egg is quite easy. Relaxing, even. And this easy-breeziness increases my confidence.

You see, oftentimes, when we work toward reaching our goals, we play the role of the sperm. We go-go-go, always zipping around, working *toward* the goal. But the egg is an important alternate mindset that is always available to you.

On your money journey, the Universe is ready and waiting to help you. Which sometimes requires that you step aside and let things happen. If you constantly take on the *spermy* role, then you never relax. Not only will this exhaust you, but you also miss out on opportunities for more magic in your life because you aren't taking the breaks that allow your mind to expand and explore non-obvious paths. Moments of rest rejuvenate your creative and productive soul.

As a result, life isn't as magical if you're always the sperm. You need moments where you're eggy. Imagine it: You're the egg, relaxed, chilled out, just kicking back and waiting for the money to come to you.

Now, this is not permission to be lazy and do nothing for weeks at a time. It is a strategy in which you balance between periods of intense activity and periods of pause, reflection, and rest. Where you let go of the reins and allow inspiration, magic, and money... to swim to you.

The moment I finish writing a book, I get excited to immediately start the next book. I have so many stories bouncing around inside me that I just want to *write, write, write.* I even used to feel guilty if I didn't write, like I might miss out, or scared the inspiration might vanish. I would get twitchy if my fingers weren't clicking away at the keyboard. But I burned myself out this way, and my creativity suffered.

So I now divide my energy between eggy and spermy.

And the results? I'm living a much better life. It's more balanced.

It goes something like this: When I'm writing a book, I'm spermy. I'm action-oriented. I push forward. I create. I plow forward and kick ass. But once the book is done, I become eggy. I take a break from working, and I imagine myself like a woman's egg, just sitting there, relaxed, while success comes to me in the form of customers as little sperm swimming up to buy my products.

Crazy? Oh yeah. These pictures in my mind drive my life. And instead of just telling myself to *relax* or *chill out*, it has a stronger impact when I imagine myself as the egg, with all the sperm rushing to me, their wiggly tails wrapped around bundles of cash for me.

Of course, not all jobs allow this kind of variable intensity, but it's not that uncommon either. Software teams work in "sprints." Entrepreneurs and corporate types often have projects with a beginning and end. The point is, it can be good for you to take a little rest between projects. Not necessarily in a hammock on the beach somewhere, but just dialing down the intensity a bit, maybe adding more reading to your day, even if it's work-related. Your creativity and big-picture thinking will likely improve, and you might even find that your average productivity increases despite the rests.

ZOOM OUT: What does this strange image of little spermies wiggling around an egg have to do with confidence?

Everything!

You see, in order to embrace the eggy mindset... it requires *confidence*. Lack of fear that you'll fall behind, or miss out on something. Being eggy tells your brain that you are not living in scarcity. That you have an abundance of time. Remember, a farmer plants seeds and then waits as they grow and produce yields. This is the same idea.

So, do your work like a sperm, and then flip it, become an egg, and rest. Be confident that, by resting, you let the energy that you put out there come back to you in the form of a great, big, fat payday.

The time to relax is when you don't have time for it.

— SYDNEY J. HARRIS

4. Dress for Mega Success

It sounds cliché, but *dressing for success* actually works... but not in the '80s "power dressing" sense. Here's the 2020's spin: In today's tech-billionaire-wearing-hoodies world, dressing for success is no longer about impressing others...

It's about presenting a deliberate self-image *to you.*

When you dress with *intention* (even if it's not "dressy"), you know you've put effort into yourself. If I show up to my laptop wearing my old sweatpants, a greasy face, and my hair looking like it went to a party while I slept, that impacts my vibe. But when I dress with intention—even if that just means I put on my special pink "work" sweatpants (yay elastic waistbands!)—then it creates a mental state targeted at *performance.* And then it's easier to slide right into where I left off the day before. Do this consistently, every day, and you'll do better work, and success will be easier to attain.

It's not unlike the mindsetting practice of making your bed every morning. In the bestselling book, *Make Your Bed: Little Things That Can Change Your Life... And Maybe the World,* Admiral William H. McRaven explains how making your bed in the morning helps you have a better day, because you're starting out your day in control. He writes, *"It demonstrated my discipline. It showed my attention to detail."*

Putting on an empowering outfit is low-hanging fruit. An easy way to start off on the right foot in the morning, in the right mental state. Put a bit of effort into your appearance, and you put a bit of pep into your prosperity step.

Money Self-Talk Script

I am power. I am success. Of course!

I operate under the belief that money comes to me just because it can. Just because I am worthy. Of course! Of course! Of course!

My secret to confidence is persistence. I show up every day for myself. For my life. I earn with ease. Yes, please! I'm in my element, and I glow.

My gifts and work are of the highest value, and I'm worthy of massive compensation. It is my right to think this way. It is my right to feel this amazing.

I just have fun, and the money comes. It's time to own it. Lightning in a bottle, here I come.

I live my life with confidence and a can-do attitude, because I do anything I put my heart and mind to. Of course!

I love my rich life. I am dazzled by my own competencies. I am capable. I am grateful and transformed.

I am worthy of everything I want. We all are.

My inner voice directs my thoughts and my life. My inner voice loves me. My inner voice tells me to go for gold!

I honor the unfolding, I welcome the surrender, I'm filled with excitement. I love feeling the wonder.

I am kind, and generous, and full of colorful love.

I start my day with a bang! I dress for success, and I put my best foot forward. I am worth it. This is just one easy way I take action.

My life is as amazing as I want it to be. I am glowing and growing every day. To the stars I go!

I am grateful for my confidence and knowing that I control it. I am in charge.

I love the excitement of the known and the unknown. I ride it like the rainbow rollercoaster ride it is. Squeeeeeal!

Exercise

Which of the ideas in this chapter resonated with you the most? Which tip will you try first and why?

CHAPTER 20

PROSPEROUS CAREERS

Only by thinking prosperity and abundance can you realize the abundant, prosperous life.

— O.S. Marden

Steve Jobs once said,

The only way to do great work is to love what you do. If you haven't found it yet, keep looking. Don't settle. As with all matters of the heart, you'll know when you find it.

When you love what you do for work, it means you enjoy it. And when you enjoy it, it means you have extra happiness. If you're not feeling joy or satisfaction from your current job, or if you feel like you're worth more than you're being paid, then evaluate your career and what you really want. Get expansive in your thinking, and decide the *theme* you want for your life.

For me, the theme I wanted was very clear: freedom. Perhaps your theme is changing the world. Or love. Or adventure. And once you've chosen your theme, then get specific, and think about how you'd envision a typical day in your dream life.

The following exercise will help. And if you already love your career, thinking about these questions can still help you get more out of it.

Answer the following:

Where are you currently in your career? Where do you want to be in your career and why?

What are three things you can do to improve your current job right now?

What can you do to improve your knowledge about your job?

Who can you talk to about moving up in the organization?

_____

_____

_____

Who can you speak with for general career guidance? Do you know someone who is already doing something that you'd like to do? If so, reach out to that person to meet for coffee or online.

_____

_____

_____

How could you explore opportunities for making a lateral move, such as a higher-paying job at a different firm in your field?

_____

_____

_____

What are your favorite hobbies and activities? List three.

_____

_____

_____

What are three of your strongest skills?

What are three skills you would enjoy acquiring or improving?

What is something you would like to create and why?

Describe your dream job.

What is preventing you from doing your dream job? Do you need more education? If so, will self-instruction suffice, or do you need a specific degree? Or perhaps a single class or certificate for some specific skill?

Who can you talk to about this dream you have?

What are some different paths you're willing to consider?

What parts of your current life are you willing to change, or let go of, in order to improve your career?

What books can you read that will inspire you to take the next steps? Are there any "how to" books to help plan your new, exciting career?

Money Self-Talk

For the Money Self-Talk in this chapter, I share three different scripts to choose from, depending on your situation:

- Employee
- Executive/manager
- Entrepreneur/business owner

Empowered Employee

If you work for somebody else, then this Money Self-Talk script is for you. Whether you like your job or not, when you change your mindset to one full of confidence and a can-do attitude, opportunities spin around you like planets around the sun. You have the power. You have the potential.

If you don't like your job, or your boss, or your coworkers, then it's time to make a change. And that change starts with *you*. Your mindset. It means putting words in your head and heart about loving yourself and... wait for it... *sending love to your job and coworkers*. Trust me. Just do it, and watch what happens. You become less bitter, less irritated, less pessimistic. You start to find more value in the company and your coworkers, you find new things to appreciate, and this makes you happier while you're still at this job. And you'll start to see new opportunities, either in your company or somewhere else, where your talents and energy would be put to better use, more appreciated, and better compensated.

Derek Lin tells a story in *The Tao of Daily Living*...

There was a man who went to see a wise sage, and the man complained that his employer did not appreciate his work. The wise sage advised the man to go back to work and learn everything he could about the job, such that there would come a time when he can leave this company, having learned a lot and go somewhere else.

Some time passed, and the man returned to visit the wise sage again. The wise sage asked the man how the plan was proceeding, and when the man planned to leave the company.

But the man no longer wished to leave because he was no longer bitter.

"And why are you no longer resentful toward your boss," the wise sage asked.

The man replied that his boss was constantly complementing him on all the new things he was learning, and for his new go-getter attitude about the company. His boss was appreciating everything about this employee, because he was going above and beyond.

Sometimes you can be overlooked at your job and feel resentment. But instead of blaming others, the first thing you should always do is take a look at yourself and your actions. *Are you showing up and doing a great job? Are you going above and beyond, if you want "above and beyond" recognition?*

When you're an epic employee, you become more valuable to the company and the people you work for. The following Money Self-Talk script focuses on transforming yourself into an epic employee and boosting your confidence for doing a job well-done.

Money Self-Talk

I love my job, and my job loves me. I am full of love and confidence, and it shines from me when I'm at work.

I contribute valuable skills and information to my team. My boss appreciates my work. My boss loves my work!

I love helping grow the company I work for. I love learning about new parts of the company, because it increases my value and allows me to help more.

I am worthy of great compensation.

I am grateful for my job. So very, very grateful.

I am an incredible employee, and I set an example for others.

I appreciate the members of my team, and they appreciate me.

I have opportunities at my job for more money and more growth, and I show up for them.

I climb the corporate ladder with ease, because I am capable.

I have ideas whirring around inside me to help the company. My talents are appreciated.

I learn from my fellow employees. They surround me and help me grow.

I have purpose in my life. I have unlimited potential. I'm going after what I want and deserve.

I am extremely grateful for my job, and I show up to work every day, ready for an amazing adventure.

Extraordinary Executive & Manager

If you are an executive or a manager of a team, then this Money Self-Talk script is for you. Or maybe you want to be promoted into a management role. This is perfect for getting you into the mindset. Remember, with self-talk, you speak about the future as if it has already happened, in the present tense. This helps you picture yourself in that role, today.

It's important to be an open-minded team leader who pays attention to the employees you manage. You know the expression: *You're only as strong as your weakest link.* This Money Self-Talk script is about being a spectacular team leader who lifts up the members of your team... which, in turn, lifts you up too.

Money Self-Talk Script

I am a rockstar manager, and I love my direct reports.

I am an open-minded team leader, and my team loves coming to me with new ideas.

I love my team, and my team loves me. We have powerful synergy, and we do an amazing job together.

I respect my team, and my team respects me. I trust the people I work with, and they trust me.

I love giving credit where credit is due, and I am quick to praise any helpful contribution from one of my team members.

As a manager, I understand that my main job is to empower my employees. I support them, allowing them to excel and succeed.

I am enthusiastic to inspire my team and everyone around me, including me!

Working with others and helping them grow is a beautiful experience. I rejoice in the success of the employees I manage.

I inspire the people who work with me, and I like helping them make their dreams come true.

I believe in me. I believe in the people who work with me.

I radiate peace in my management style. My team is incredible. I lead my team with confidence and ease, and we all respect each other.

I am grateful for my position and honored to be in my role.

Leading people is fulfilling, and I am inspired to inspire others.

Epic Entrepreneur & Business Owner

This Money Self-Talk script is for business owners and the trail-blazing entrepreneur, or anybody who wants to be one! Use it to fill your powerful mind with images of the freedom of being your own boss, acquiring customers or clients, and growing your business to soaring heights.

Money Self-Talk

I'm an amazing entrepreneur. I am full of great ideas. Only greatness lies before me.

I love owning my time, and I get to do that as an entrepreneur. I love my freedom!

I have a phenomenal memory. I have an eye for details. I have the ability to think big, as big as the night sky.

Owning my own company is an incredible experience, and I am grateful for this opportunity.

Getting new clients and customers is effortless. I attract them with my powerful, elevated energy.

I love my business ideas. I am building my dreams into my reality. I am awesome. I am freedom. I soar.

The people who work with me love working with me. And I love working with them. I am grateful for these relationships.

I am a happy, intuitive entrepreneur. It's easy for me to attract and hire the most amazing, skilled employees. I use my intuition to make the best choices.

I rejoice in the prosperity of others. We're all popping! We're all lit. Come on! Let's all do this!

I'm here for my blow-off-the-rooftop life! I'm an epic entrepreneur, of course!

Clients chase me down, throwing money my way, and it's the most rewarding feeling.

My business is amazing. My customers are amazing. I am amazing. The whole world is amazing.

Exercise

If you haven't already done so, write down your answers in the spaces provided with the questions at the beginning of this chapter.

CHAPTER 21

THE GREAT "THANK YOU" EXPERIMENT

Imagination is everything. It is the preview of life's coming attractions.

— ALBERT EINSTEIN

Gratitude is your *secret sauce* when it comes to manifesting.

Gratitude's power lies in instantly transforming your vibe and uplifting your mood... which helps you attract and see more of what you want. Such as money. But it can also be so much more. It can help you find epic joy.

How is gratitude so powerful? Because gratitude makes you fully present when depression might drag you into the past, or anxiety might yank you into the future with worries. Gratitude makes you immediately realize *how rich you already are*. Gratitude will always boost your spirit, no matter what, when, or where. That's why gratitude is a foundational part of living your epic life.

The Great "Thank You" Experiment

I once conducted a gratitude experiment where I went through an entire day full of gratitude. You might be thinking... um, big deal... How is that a major experiment? But it *was* a big deal! Because, when you shift your focus like this for an entire day, it's some *serious* gratitude. So serious that I dubbed it my *Fierce-as-Shit Gratitude Day*. But if you prefer, you can call it your *Thank You Day*.

During the experiment, gratitude was the focus of pretty much every thought I had for an entire day. This meant that I gave gratitude for everything—*good or not!* And let me tell you, I had no idea that it would turn out as profound as it did. It took me to a new level in my magical living. A *cosmic* level. And the results were so staggeringly awesome, that this exercise became a monthly feature in my life.

So here's what the entire day looks like... here's exactly how I did it:

Are you ready?

I simply said "thank you"... *for everything.*

That's all I did.

It might seem insignificant, but here's the thing... when I say "everything," I mean *everything.* I said thank you for waking up. I said thank you for my feet as I padded to the bathroom that morning. I thanked my toothbrush and my toothpaste. I thanked my tongue while brushing my teeth (ok, that one was weird). I thanked my coffee and my coffee cup. And the water, kitchen, and coffee pot. I thanked the window as I looked outside while the coffee brewed. I thanked the dogs, the furniture, the walls of the house, the palm trees and humming birds outside, the roof, the laptop, the iPhone. I even thanked the door to the garage.

Do you get the picture? I thanked everything around me, everything I saw. I wrapped all of them in love, as if these things were the most treasured things in my life. *"I see you, lampshade, and I blanket you in love. I see you, pine tree, and I wrap you in love. Thank you. Thank you."*

And here's where it gets even weirder. I even thanked the not-so-good stuff. On this particular day, I wasn't running advertising for our business, because the cost was too high, but... wait for it... *I gave thanks for that.* And when I helped my daughter make her bed, and I saw crumbs in her bed, I thanked the crumbs, too. I had a headache and thanked it. *This is weird right?*

How ridiculous does this sound?

Giving thanks for things *I don't even like?*

Does this mean I'll attract more things that I don't like? *Ha!* I know better. That's not even possible. When you give thanks to things, you no longer feel sad or mad. You only experience elevated emotions. When I do this, some of my heightened emotions feel downright silly, for the mere act of what I was doing. And that's a good thing. It means I'm still attracting my richest life.

Gratitude is greatness. And you can come alive with it! It puts you in control of your life. When you give thanks for a struggle or a mishap, then you're automatically not letting it *bother* you. When you radiate shimmering appreciation, you simply emit a better, more powerful vibe.

Boyfriend dump you? *Thanks!*

Lose your purse? *Thanks!*

Got a flu or a migraine? *Thanks!*

I know, crazy, right? But remember, it's always, *always* about your vibe —*your energy.* And gratitude is your winning ticket to expressing this good vibration consistently, to help your dreams come true. Your brain can only focus on one thing at a time. So when you focus on things you're grateful for, you block bad feelings, and they no longer run the show inside your head. *You get to choose* that everything is good, even if somebody else might think that something is bad. It's a mindset, and gratitude is the new sheriff in town.

"Thank You Day" Tips:

Try it! Pick one day this month, and do this all day long. No matter what happens, go crazy-crackers with your gratitude.

- **Pick Your Day** – Select one day a month for your *Thank You Day,* and set it to repeat on your calendar. I like the first day of every month to set the tone for the whole month.

- **Things to Thank** – On your chosen day, your goal is to say thank you as much as possible. The best way to do this is when you're waiting for something else. For example, if the coffee is brewing, instead of looking at my phone, I look around my environment and say thank you for everything I see. If I'm at a red light, the same. If I walk from one room to the next, the same. If I'm waiting for my computer to do something, the same. If you're stirring chili on the stove, waiting for the garage door to go up, or taking a second to scratch your calf, the same: Say thank you for something. You're not doing this when you're actually doing other things, like reading or working. But if you're writing an email, you can say thank you to the email once you hit *send.* Be sure to say the name of the thing you're thanking. This gives the statement more meaning and more *oomph.* So, instead of looking at my hands and saying, "Thank you," I say, "Thank you, *hands.*"

- **Whisper the Words** – You get an extra splash of good vibes when you say the words out loud. Whispering is fine and great. I love doing this, because it's like the thing I'm thanking *hears it.* It makes it more intimate between me and the thing. But let me tell you, sometimes I throw my hands up hallelujah-style and sing in my best opera voice,

"Thaaaaank youuuuu!" This makes me snort with laughter, and even more love pours out of me, like a dam has been smashed open, and a flood of hearts pours out.

- **Reminder Notes** – The trick to making this gratitude day work is actually remembering to do it. Sticky notes to the rescue! On my day of gratitude, I post sticky notes everywhere to remind myself to keep being grateful for everything. After a while, it becomes habit, and it feels natural and wonderful when you respond to everything with "Thank you!"

Real Benefits from This Mindset

We can become frustrated or annoyed with the things that bother us. Or... we can thank them. I thanked the crumbs. I thanked my stubbed toe. I even thanked COVID for sweeping through our home and dancing with me. Because life is better when we choose to be grateful—by even the most mundane, crazy, and seemingly awful things. I found a silver lining in each one of these annoyances. Always remember:

How we choose to respond matters more than our circumstances.

Gratitude Plus Money Self-Talk

When you use gratitude to help build future prosperity, it does something magical to your efforts. It sprinkles pixie dust on the whole project, in two ways. For starters, gratitude puts you in a better mood, because you're grateful for what you have, and it's important to include lines of self-talk about gratitude in your script for this purpose. That's what the whole Thank You experiment is about: changing your vibe by being grateful for what you have.

But there's a second way to use gratitude with your Money Self-Talk... for drawing your future desires to you. How do you give gratitude for something you don't yet possess? You pretend you *do* possess it. True, you don't actually have those desires manifested yet, but you visualize yourself having them to train your brain and keep your focus on helping you see and find opportunities to manifest those desires.

When you feel gratitude as if you've already obtained your desires (such as by using present tense self-talk), it's like your brain thinks it's already happened. So when I'm doing my Money Self-Talk, I thank the future car I'll have... *as if I have it parked in my garage now.* I visualize myself going into the garage and seeing it, loving it, and appreciating it. I do the same for anything I want to draw into my life, whether it's health, love, success, or material things like a new laptop, or a swimming pool.

For this reason, some of the lines about gratitude in your Money Self-Talk script need to be personalized to address your specific desires, because we all want different things. And so the following Money Self-Talk script is deliberately generic, in order to be used by anyone, but you'll want to add a few lines specific to the things you want. Blank spaces have been provided in the script for this purpose.

Go beyond just being grateful for money coming into your life, and add some self-talk about the things you want to *do* with the money. For instance, you can add affirmations about the things you want to *buy* with the money. Think of your desires, and think about how much money you want in order to have those things.

This specificity makes it easier to feel excitement and gratitude because you paint a picture in your mind of how you'll use the money, which makes it more concrete and real.

For example, an affirmation for $500,000 is fun, sure. But if you knew you were going to use the $500,000 for a new home, then you'd want to write something like:

> *Thank you $500,000. I'm buying my new*
> *cabin in Montana and filling it with rustic furniture.*

Money Self-Talk Script

Thank you, life. Thank you, energy! Thank you, money-money-money!

Thank you, health. Thank you, wealth.

Thank you bank account filled with overflowing cash that's always coming my way.

Thank you, love. I love love. Thank you, healing world.

I'm grateful for all the food I have. I'm grateful for my body that exercises and moves.

Thank you, fun. Thank you, laughter. You make my soul sing.

Thank you, beautiful weather, earth and sky. Thank you, life and living.

Thank you for my easy life and effortless living.

I am grateful for my creativity, because I am a creative genius.

I am grateful for everything. Every single thing.

Thank you, gratitude. I am in love with life, thank you.

Thank you for my cash. And my teeth! Thank you for my investments. And my feet!

Thank you for my relaxed mindset. I am calm.

Thank you for my beautiful friends, cranky neighbors, and wacky family members.

I am empowered with pizazz and shine, thank you. I am grateful for my incredible, magical mindset. It makes me happy. I am so grateful for everything I have. My life is sublime.

I am grateful for my (insert something you desire) _____.

I am grateful for my (insert something you desire) _____.

I am grateful for my (insert something you desire) _____.

I am grateful for my (insert something you desire) _____.

(Note: Refer to the Montana example above for the following.)

Thank you, (thing)_____. I'm _____

_____.

Thank you, (thing)_____. I'm _____

_____.

Thank you, (thing)_____. I'm _____

_____.

Thank you, (thing)_____. I'm _____

_____.

Exercise

Reflect on the role of gratitude in your life and how it relates to your prosperity journey. Spend a few minutes writing about what you're grateful for, both big and small, and include as many things as the space permits. The idea is to list so many items that you train your brain to think about gratitude often.

CHAPTER 22

EAT YOUR DAMN LIVER

Most people tiptoe through life trying to make it safely to death.

— Bob Proctor

There are times when you're working toward your money goals, and you just need to do what needs to be done, even if you absolutely don't feel like it. In other words...

Eat your damn liver.

When you're on this journey to prosperity, there might be steps you need to take that are about as appetizing as a *steaming pile of liver*. And if you're like most people, that means doing steps that you don't love doing. Because, who really likes liver? (If you happen to like it, just substitute into this metaphor some healthy food that you despise. Broccoli maybe?)

I'm here to tell ya, you have to eat your liver. Figuratively. In other words, *just do it*. Eat your liver. Do not procrastinate. Do not put off steps you need to take. Eat your liver. Put on your big girl (or big boy) pants and do what you're supposed to do. *Eat your damn liver!*

That's how I look at the things I have to do, but I don't want to. It could be as simple as taking the first step on a project. Or that one phone call you need to make to get the ball rolling.

Many writers speak about the dreaded "blank page," in which the act of writing the first word can seem so difficult that they'll do anything to avoid it.

I have my own version of this well-known writer's demon, but instead of not knowing what to write about, I have the opposite problem. Sometimes I have so many words and ideas bouncing around in my brain that I can't imagine how to make sense of them all, and I don't know where to begin. At times like this, procrastination becomes a tantalizing temptress. *Oh, I'll first follow up with people on social media. Oh, I'll check email. Oh, I'll make my daughter lunch. Oh, I'll alphabetize my spice rack. Wait, is that a piece of fuzz on the floor?... I'd better vacuum the whole house.*

But no, that's not me. I don't give in.

Why? Because I eat my damn liver.

I'm a badass, and I get the job done.

Are there things I don't want to do? Absolutely! *But I do them anyway.* When it comes to writing my books, I sit my butt down, and I write my words. Even if I've got nada in my skull. I just start typing. Even if it's gibberish that comes out of me. I eat my liver.

If you want it to work, you must do the work.

Magical Thoughts to Make Liver Yummy

Would you believe that there's a way to make this liver taste better? You can do it... with your thoughts. By changing the dialogue in your head about the things you have to do, you make them easier to get done. And you do this by saying that you "love doing" the thing you're going to do. Oh yes, I'm quite serious. Love. Not "like." Not "tol-erate." LOVE.

For example, do you have to go to the dentist, which you detest so much that you'd rather give your ex-husband a pedicure? Then simply say out loud,

*I **love** going to the dentist.*

Say it a dozen times a day so it takes root, starting a few days out from your appointment. And say it anytime the appointment happens to enter your mind.

Do you want to start some project that has the potential to change your financial circumstances, but you've been putting it off? Perhaps creating a budget, or a side income, or hunting for a better job? Or finally writing that novel you've dreamed about for ten years?

Whatever it is, break it down into tiny steps, and then focus only on the first step. If it were the novel example, perhaps that first step is to simply jot down a rough outline. And if this is hard, if you find it intimidating, you'd say to yourself, over and over,

*I **love** writing my outline.*

In fact, go even bigger and sing it! Throw your hands up in the air with joy at every liver-filled step you need to take. Be proud! Be tough! Be a badass! Go over the top! Do it! Do it!

And then feel the magic.

Feel how it totally softens the initial resistance. It makes the liver easier to get down.

That's what the following script is about: getting you pumped to do the things that taste like liver to you. So, the next time you're tasked with doing something you're not excited about, pull out this script, and read it a few times to boost yourself up.

Money Self-Talk Script

I'm a badass, and I get the job done. I love _____ and I'm in charge!

I can do anything when I have the right language about it. This even makes it fun!

I see myself blasting through my day, powered by my own badassedness. Yes! That's me... I believe!

Doing _____ is easy and fun. I'm on fire. I'm on point. I get it done.

My mind is powerful, and I'm the master conductor of my life.

The positive words I speak and think create my great energy and experience. I love owning my actions... owning my feelings... owning my life!

I feel aliveness in each moment, no matter what I'm doing, and that includes _____.

I choose confidence. I choose love. I choose ME!

I am full of dazzling enthusiasm for every step I take and everything I do.

I am abundant. I am strong. I will myself to do it all.

I open my wings, spread them wide, 'cuz I'm gonna fly. I fly through doing _____ with sparkles and fire in my eyes.

I am secure. I am a bold believer. I am making magic happen. I am a joyful force full of life!

I pat my own back for a job well done. I show myself what I'm made of every day. I win, and I won.

I know my every strength. I shine, shine, shine. I make more money every day, because I show up and get the JOB DONE.

I am worthy of a rich life, full of texture, and love, and fun. That's why I get the job done.

Exercises

Think about something you really should do, but you don't want to, and you've made excuses to procrastinate. Write the thing down, and write down the excuses. And no cheating, write them all!

Next, change your self-talk about the thing you didn't want to do by telling yourself *you love doing it*. Write it down five times, and remember to use first person present tense. Then say it out loud. Heck, sing and dance it a few times! And then repeat it some more.

CHAPTER 23

SIMPLICITY FOR SATISFACTION

As you simplify your life, the laws of the universe will be simpler.

— Henry David Thoreau

Let's ponder the idea of the word, *satisfaction.*

People often set goals about happiness, and you can absolutely create a more cheerful and happy outlook with your self-talk. I work on this every day. In fact, it's one of my most important life skills, managing my emotional state... you know... being happy. But have you ever felt the awesome feeling of *satisfaction*? Like, really feeling satisfied with your life?

After I attained some big financial goals—we paid off our debt, saved money, invested money, and we were ready to buy a home—I was at a point where I had the option of living a life that was a bit splashy and extravagant... or, I could create a life that was simpler. Where I had fewer material possessions, less going on, and more free time. And I realized that, in the latter scenario, I had more control and more freedom.

As I've said a few times now, freedom is one of my core driving values. Freedom to own my schedule. Freedom with my day. And I asked myself, *What would it take to be that way? What would my life look like if I had total freedom over my schedule and control over my projects?*

I realized that I could create a more secure and financially bullet-proof life... if I chose a simpler life. A life where I was satisfied with what I had, and that didn't mean a big, fancy house or a luxury car. Don't get me wrong, those things are great if you want them. They're beautiful!

But I didn't. Not anymore.

I was finding that I was more satisfied with simpler living. I was still into quality, to be sure, but I just wanted... less.

A bit *minimalist*, even.

And I was loving this notion, as it brought a strange feeling of satisfaction. One I'm not sure I had ever really concentrated on before. Maybe because I thought minimalism meant living a lesser life... as in, good *enough*, but not more.

But nothing could be farther from the truth!

Here's the thing about satisfaction the way I mean it: It's an undeniable and wholesome feeling. No, it's not glittery and sparkly like happiness. But it's strong. It's backbone. It's stability. Peace. Of. Mind.

Happiness is an emotional state. It comes and goes, depending on the situation. It can be fleeting.

Satisfaction is the long-term version. It's not fleeting.

Satisfaction endures.

I loved this idea. It was as though I had reached a point where I had done such a great job building up my self-esteem with my self-talk, and I had evolved to a point where I attained some big goals, which led to becoming confident and very satisfied with life in general.

Opting for simplicity wasn't "settling," it was choosing a different way to live.

I was ready to make this profound shift. I felt satisfied with everything we had. I found myself drawn to simpler things. Less clutter, for instance. A life with more nature, which meant moving to a state with lots of trees and outdoor living. A life of security. A life where I didn't need to work for weeks or months if I didn't want to. A life where I had complete freedom with projects and work. Now that's ABUNDANCE to me!

Prosperity doesn't always have to mean *more-more-more* when it comes to money and possessions. The trick to living well really is figuring out what makes you ultimately satisfied, and then, once you attain that, sitting there comfortably and securely. It's an incredible position of power for living one's life. It's fine to keep striving, reaching, and growing... but not from a place of shifting goalposts and perpetual scarcity, where no amount of success is ever enough.

It's a little tricky. We are wired to recalibrate when things change. To normalize our gains, causing us to want more. Psychologists call this the *hedonic treadmill,* and it's why some people own ten Lamborghinis or hundreds of designer handbags. On one hand, I hesitate to judge... *you do you,* right? On the other hand... really? Will handbag number 487 finally scratch that itch?

Simplicity is so much... well, simpler.

It used to be a bit bold to say "I want less" in a world that places so much importance on status, and where advertisers train us to gauge happiness by constantly comparing ourselves to our neighbors or our sister-in-law.

But in recent years, there's been a generational shift, as millennials (who are now entering their forties!), often choose to go without things like car ownership, or talk about minimalism and living in "tiny houses," or emphasizing experiences like travel and cooking over the accumulation of cheaply made junk they don't want to see end up in a landfill one day.

I'm not a millennial (I'm Gen X), but I get it. I don't want to live in a tiny house, but I don't want a mansion, either. Oh gawd, imagine the vacuuming!

You want to figure out what really makes your heart sing.

For me, that's freedom and nature. And I love this way of living. As I put the final touches on this book, I'm in a little cabin on a remote lake in northern Michigan, and I watch the mallards and loons on the water all day long. I feel abundance beyond measure. Total peace of mind.

I am content.

Will I keep working? Writing? Yes! I love it. I wake up each morning and relax into my day. I walk in the woods anytime I want, multiple times a day. I choose what to do and when. I have way less stress and anxiety because I have more control. I'm healthier because I have the time to do healthy things.

That's simple living.

That's *rich* living.

So when you're living your life of radical abundance and juicy prosperity, ask yourself if you have enough, or if you want more. And if you want more, then *go for it*. Keep your energy high and have fun!

But sometimes, we change in the middle of the journey, and that's great, too. In the beginning, I was all about the glam, and then shortly after, I was like, "Oh, that was fun, but now I want something different. *I want simplicity.*"

In the famous words of Paris Hilton, "*That's hot.*"

Money Self-Talk Script

I am destined for the most beautiful life of my design.

I embrace simplicity. I appreciate the thousands of small, wonderful things in my daily life.

Simplicity creates abundance and space for happiness to flourish in my life.

Life is full of brilliant color, and I have the time to appreciate it all.

When I wake up every morning, I am calm and content. All is well.

I find delight in life's little pleasures, like savoring a cup of delicious coffee, and feeling the sunshine on my face. I walk through my day noticing new things all the time, because I have the time to do this.

I have freedom of schedule, freedom in my day. I get to choose what I do.

I release unnecessary complications, and this makes my spirit light and breezy.

I fall asleep with peace of mind, because I have all that I need and more.

When I simplify my life, I take charge and make a playful atmosphere that invites laughter, creativity, and abundance.

I accept and allow myself to expand my mind bigger than ever before.

Today, I choose to simplify my thoughts, which sharpens my focus. This helps bring abundance, prosperity, and joy.

I know that when I keep my mind high and bright, it glows with intention, and I see the way to the greatest life ever.

Simple living brings me clarity of thought, which allows me to flow and unleash my creativity.

I am inspired beyond belief. My life is full of riches. I have an abundance of time to do everything I want.

Exercise

Acquiring large amounts of money requires doing things differently than most people... otherwise, most people would be wealthy. *You doing you*—that is, doing your own thing, in your own way, rather than copying what everybody else is doing—is what will bring you ultimate happiness and satisfaction. What does doing things differently mean to you personally?

CHAPTER 24

INCREDIBLE INVESTING MINDSET

The rich don't work for money. They make money work for them.

— ROBERT KIYOSAKI

Investing is ultimately the most powerful way to build wealth. The amount of time you can work is limited, whereas money and income-producing assets *make money for you*, even while you sleep!

And even people who make millions from their jobs or businesses, well, they just turn around and invest those millions to multiply their wealth ten times or more.

I personally found the prospect of investing substantial sums of money to be both exciting and daunting. Part of me was thrilled with the idea, because, you know, the whole money-in-your-sleep thing. Abundance where I don't really have *to do* anything... *woohoo!* I invest money, and the companies I invest in do the rest. I mean, let's be real... as much as I love earning money as an entrepreneur, I love the idea of dividend income, too.

But the other part of me felt overwhelmed about investing, which wasn't an uplifting feeling, because there was so much uncertainty and unknown.

So I took matters into my mind's own hands. First, I created my investment mindset—*even while I was still in debt.* I changed the language in my brain, and I prepared myself, because I knew there'd come a time when I would have the means to invest. In other words, I wasn't making investments yet, but I was including lines in my Money Self-Talk that helped *make that my reality.*

I also started learning about investing before I had money to invest. I assumed I'd have a mix of stocks, index funds, and maybe real estate, but I didn't know much about them. But that's okay, because I live a *Learning Lifestyle,* right? (See chapter 16.) So I grabbed my journal and made notes about the things I could do to accomplish my investment-learning goals, and I wrote self-talk about this, too. I started reading books, and I would eventually hire a professional wealth manager. But I never stopped learning on my own, and I subscribed to a couple of great investing newsletters, which keep me updated on the latest trends.

I learned that during the pandemic, CVS Pharmacy was doing well because of all the people going into the stores for the shot, and doing some shopping while they were there. Little stories like this make perfect sense, but they hadn't occurred to me. But after hearing many such stories, week after week, you start to learn things and notice patterns, which you can then use to make smarter investment decisions.

You can use your Money Self-Talk to support this type of pattern recognition and learn it like any skill, to make connections when you see other news events, or new technologies (such as AI), and position yourself, your business, and your investments to take advantage of them in the future.

Investing wisely requires emotional discipline. And the more involved you are, the more discipline it requires. That is, people who stick a percentage of their paycheck into a mutual fund and rarely check it (which isn't a bad idea)... they don't require emotional discipline because they aren't actively engaged with the process. But someone on the other end of the engagement spectrum—day trading on the latest news, market movements, and hunches—this person needs to manage their emotions to make sure they don't take over. Markets are driven by cycles of fear and greed, and the best approach for the active investor is to let neither of these emotions rule the day.

> *Be fearful when others are greedy, and greedy when others are fearful.*
>
> — WARREN BUFFET

We humans also have a tendency to ascribe our successes to skill, and our failures to bad luck. In reality, many successes and failures are a combination of both of these ingredients.

So whether you're irrationally exuberant, or irrationally scared, or underestimating your abilities, or overestimating them, you can use your Money Self-Talk to take control of the fear and ego centers of your brain, to make you an extremely cool, calm, self-aware investor.

Money Self-Talk Script

I make money work for me. My investments earn money for me while I sleep.

I naturally find success with investments. I am confident with my investments, and I love how my investments appreciate.

I love investing, and investing loves me. I'm an excellent steward of my investments.

Crazy interest rates or whacked out inflation? They don't faze me. I easily surf the waves of any economy.

I am worthy of owning assets that grow in value over time.

I love buying things that make me money. It's fun. Making smart investments comes naturally to me.

My net worth grows, and grows, and grows!

I make great investments because I'm open-minded, and opportunities present themselves to me all the time.

I luxuriate in financial peace as I drift to sleep each night. My dreams are full of ideas for ventures.

I love investing my money, and I make smart choices about where to put my money.

I have multiple streams of income, and I am grateful for my expanding net worth.

I don't let my emotions guide my investments. I expect highs and lows, and I'm cool, calm, and collected, because I know I'll do well over the long-term.

I am at peace with my portfolio and excited about it growing and growing.

I am worthy of investment abundance. I am worthy of the money I earn.

I ride the market's ups and downs with grace. Over time, my thoughtful, diversified investments steadily build my net worth.

I tap into my intuition when making investment decisions.

The unknown is part of my life, and I love it. It's exciting!

Exercise

If you're new to investing, what are some ways you could learn more about it? Or if you're already knowledgeable, how could you increase your knowledge? Perhaps subscribe to a newsletter, or listen to one podcast per week on the topic, or study one particular industry or company. List as many ideas as you can think of.

CHAPTER 25

POWERING THROUGH TOUGH TIMES

Never promote someone who hasn't made some bad mistakes; you would be promoting someone who hasn't done much.

— HERBERT DOW

Your journey with prosperity can be a roller coaster ride, full of jaw-dropping, stomach-spinning fun. But not everyone likes roller coasters. That said, it doesn't mean that the downs can't be exhilarating and exciting, or at least useful teachers.

You might have days where you feel stretched more than you're comfortable with. You might have epic failures, or you might have a thousand tiny mistakes. And through it all, your job is to keep your emotions elevated and confident... always up and always on, as much as you can. Moving forward, forward, forward. When it rains, you grab your umbrella and splash in the puddles. You don't whine or complain, because that's a victim mentality, and you are not a victim. *You're a hero!*

As author Richard Bach said,

Argue for your limitations, and sure enough, they're yours.

Your mission is to keep your spirit elevated. Have a confident mindset and deep belief that everything *works out for you*. Say that over and over. Say it every day! I do!

You thrive, and you don't let setbacks mean anything negative about you, your capabilities, or your future. Remember, tough and wonky circumstances make you smarter and stronger. They strengthen your resolve and resilience.

A Shift in Perception

If things ever get tough, here's a tip:

Change your ***perception about*** your circumstances.

If something bad happens, learn to process it without falling into a hole of negativity. Find any way possible to view it *through a hero's eyes*. All heroes have setbacks, right? Do you know why? Because without setbacks, they're not heroes! They're just regular Joes.

When I shift my focus like this, I don't see failures. I only see *feedback*. Feedback is useful information. Feedback is how we learn. It helps you make better decisions in the future. And good decisions are where success comes from.

Billionaire Mark Cuban says the choice is always yours... Are you going to ignore life's lessons, or learn something from them? Because if something goes bad, I promise, there will be some good from it. Every adversity has hidden within it a benefit... you just have to sniff it out. Your happiness is *never* dependent on everything going wonderfully in the world. Your happiness is a choice you make no matter what. Got that? Always remember:

Happiness is a choice.

A client canceled? Now you can focus on getting another one.

Got sick and you had to stop working on your project for two weeks? Sounds like a blessing, and you got to rest.

Catch a cold that gave you a raspy voice and cough so you can't record a new podcast episode? Looks like a great time to write down ideas for a year's worth of podcast episodes.

Didn't get the job you wanted? No problem, now you have time to increase your skills and get an even better job.

Make Your Mess Your Message & Make Money While You're at It

I know I can *always* do something with a bad experience—no matter what it is. Like *make money from it*. I take what I learn from any mistake or failure, and I can teach other people about it.

I love what Robin Robert says, *"Make your mess your message."* Let that sink in. Or Oprah Winfrey, who said, *"Turn your wounds into wisdom."*

When something goes wrong, let that be a message that you can turn into something valuable *and* help others at the same time.

Or take me, as a novelist... I look at every sad or icky experience as an opportunity to add it into a future story. I'm always ready to capitalize on new material the Universe sends my way, and it's sending you stuff, too.

An optimist is one who makes opportunities of his difficulties.

— HARRY TRUMAN

Two New Rules

Rule #1: Anytime something "bad" happens, you have one job to do: *Keep your mindset focused on your next move.* Keep your eye on the prize... the life you want. And keep looking for more opportunities.

We often think we know the way, but then life presents a different path. How's that saying go?... *"You plan. God laughs."*

There are many variations of this little tidbit of wisdom:

No plan survives first contact with the enemy.

— HELMUTH VON MOLTKE

Or my favorite,

Everyone has a plan until you get punched in the mouth.

— MIKE TYSON

So never let circumstances or unexpected changes get you down, because sometimes it's a necessary, new direction. *And a hidden opportunity to make money.*

Rule #2: Don't complain about your failures to everybody. Learn, let go, and dance on. You should be too busy planning your next steps —*and then taking action!*—to be wasting time moaning about your circumstances.

The Phoenix Suns basketball team's motto is: *Next Man Up!* If a player gets injured, do they whine and get depressed? Hell no. They all say, "Next man up." It's just part of their system. They're always prepared and ready to move on. They don't let mishaps get them down. If a star player gets hurt, sometimes a sportscaster will ask, "What are you guys going to do with so-n-so out of the next few games?" Their response, every time, is to shrug like it's no big deal. Because... *"Next man up."*

And they keep playing their best possible game, like professionals.

That's what you want to be. *A professional.* A professional at the art of living.

So if something doesn't go your way, no big deal, you get working on something else. You just keep on moving.

> *People are always blaming their circumstances for what they are. I don't believe in circumstances. The people who get on in this world are the people who get up and look for the circumstances they want, and if they can't find them, they make them.*

> — GEORGE BERNARD SHAW

Pivot Power

Consider the young entrepreneur who took a bunch of rolls of canvas to California during the 1849 gold rush, with plans to sell tents to all the miners. But when he got there, he learned that nobody needed tents because the California weather was so mild. Problem, right? So did he pack up and go home? No, he cut up his canvas and sewed the pieces into tough pairs of trousers, and he sold those to the miners instead. The man's name was Levi Strauss, the man who introduced blue jeans to the world.

You see, problems virtually always come with some kind of opportunity attached. The trick is to look for the opportunity. They're always there, but they're usually not obvious. They only reveal themselves to the clever people who *seek them out*.

At any time, you can go online and work toward another degree, never even leaving your house if you don't want to. You can learn a new skill and monetize it. In today's world, technology has made it easier than ever to succeed and make more money. You have to keep your mind confident, and your feelings elevated, and go for it! Believe in yourself. Believe in your *resourcefulness*. Trust that you will laugh at the mistakes you made along the way. And then do something about it. Strap yourself in and crack your knuckles. *It's game time!*

I have a friend who helps her husband with his remodeling contract work. She's a hardcore babe, and she helps him on the job, cutting tile, demolishing walls with a sledge hammer, and generally kicking butt. All while wearing her heavy black eyeliner and false eyelashes. But one day, she hurt her back, and the doctor said she couldn't help her husband anymore. This would mean he'd have to work slower, or hire somebody and pay that person... and she knew this would slow their progress building their wealth.

Did she let this get her down? Ha. She laughed in the face of adversity. She' clever, and she *pivoted*. In just a few days, she was enrolled in an online interior design program for home remodeling—so she could take on a *new* role for her husband! One that would improve their offers to clients by showcasing different design ideas. That's clever and resourceful. Girlfriend made *treasure out of trash.*

It doesn't matter what the world throws at you, whether it's a bad back or a global pandemic. When necessary, *you pivot.*

I am not what happened to me, I am what I choose to become.

— Carl Jung

Money Self-Talk Script

I am available for the best mindset at all times.

My fiery passion glows hot and lights my way. That's who I am, that's my life.

I am capable and resourceful. I am resilient and strong. I am a badass.

I pivot with power whenever I need to. Taking another road is always an option.

I am creative and full of ideas whenever I want them.

I keep my mind focused, and my eyes are always on the prize.

I laugh in the face of adversity—muahahahaha!

I keep my heart and mind uplifted. This is greatness. I choose greatness. I am resourceful and empowered.

I love tapping into my intuition for sparkling guidance. I close my eyes, take a breath, and feel my way to the answers. I know the way.

I have a beautiful heart, full of gratitude and love for all of my blessings.

I keep my face tipped to the sky. A smile gracing my lips.

I have a thumpin' beat in my feet, and it fills my soul. I am worthy of every money dream I have. I love me!

The tiniest, unexpected change could move my life on a completely new trajectory. I am open to all possibilities. Money, here I come!

I live each and every day with energy. My heart glimmers with gratitude. I breathe deep and powerful calm into each breath.

I am remarkable, and I'm a treasure seeker. I dig deep till I find it, no matter the circumstances.

I shift my vibe on a dime and get back on my magic carpet ride.

Exercise

It's time to reflect thoughtfully on mistakes you've made in your life. Take one or two of them, and mine them for treasure. What did you learn? How did you grow? Or how did they end up improving your life, even if they were difficult at the time?

CHAPTER 26

GOING EXTRA WOO

This world, after all our science and sciences, is still a miracle... wonderful, inscrutable, magical, and more to whosoever will think of it.

— THOMAS CARLYLE

I want to finish this book with a little chapter dedicated to opening your mind extra wide to the magic of the Universe... going *extra woo*, if you will. Because, although I talk about practical steps to prosperity, when it comes to figuring out how this awesome, crazy reality works, I can't help but wonder a huge *What if?*

I mean, like, really... what if you just had to think of what you want, and feel the magic of drawing it to you, and it'd really come?

What if there is something happening beyond what we currently understand or comprehend? What if all we had to do was place an order for abundance with the universe, like you order an omelet at a diner, and the universe just delivered? What if you sat on your couch and visualized what you wanted—and I'm talking *huge* abundance stuff—with such calm expectation that it just happened?

So have a little fun with me. I saved this chapter for last because, by now, some of the affirmations below won't seem *that* crazy. When I first started doing my Money Self-Talk, I had to get comfortable with such bold and wild affirmations. The first few times I read my script, I blushed at my audacity, but over time, it became a part of me. I started to feel worthier and worthier with every read.

Let's go full-on woo with the Money Self-Talk script in this chapter, and imagine the most *moneyest* possibilities that you desire.

I'm talking *big* ideas here...

Instead of "I want to go to Europe anytime I want..."and instead of "I want to fly first class to Europe anytime I want..." say,

> *I fly in a private jet to Europe anytime I want!*

Yeah baby, *that's right!* Let's get crazy big and be mega playful, and tickle our souls until we giggle out loud. Don't give one thought to "how" the goal or visualization could happen, because that's not part of this exercise. Just revel in the deliciousness of imagining that you have all the things you want, with the snap of your fingers. You know, full-woo stuff. :)

Okay, let's have some fun...

Money Self-Talk Script

Money is coming to me, right here and right now. Always. I have tons of money. Millions and millions of dollars.

I can take a private jet to anywhere in the world, anytime I want.

My home is full of exquisite furniture and anything I desire.

I give a million dollars to my favorite causes anytime I want.

I get the best tables at the best Michelin-starred restaurants.

I just have fun, and the money comes.

It's so easy making money. I have many different sources of income.

I am worthy of everything I want, of course! We all are!

Thank you, abundance, for being there 24 hours a day.

I sleep when I want, and I wake when I want. I own my schedule, and if I want to, I can play all day long.

I just have fun, and the money comes.

I continually experience overflow with money and riches. I'm wealthy, and I love my life.

I have anything available when I want. I always manifest more. This is who I've decided I am.

I'm on a blazing new awesome adventure with money.

Abundance is all around me. I live a life full of prosperity.

I am relaxed, having fun, and enjoying one helluva life.

I just have fun, and the money always comes.

Exercise

Imagine you're living a life filled with prosperity beyond your wildest dreams. What is that life like? How do you feel every day? Take a moment to visualize this and write about it. Add lots of juicy details. Make it as sizzling and glamorous as you desire, *and have fun!*

AFTERWORD & FREE STUFF

You now know the power you have over your finances. Over *money*. You know that it all begins with your *mindset*. And you know that you can create that mindset simply with your self-talk.

Have fun.

Be brave.

Be bold.

Make prosperity easier by embracing the magical with the practical, and show up to your life, every day, to take steps toward your goals. Use your self-talk to make the adventure more meaningful, happier, and more effective.

Decide on the true meaning of money for you, and keep your mind open to all the incredible opportunities out there that are just waiting for you. When those sparkly steps on the path catch your eye, inspiring you, *go for it*. And remember to be grateful, "eat your liver" when necessary, and see any mistakes as your epic wins.

Most importantly, *believe, believe, believe!* You are worthy of your money dreams. Use your Money Self-Talk as the foundation of it all.

Think crazy and amazing thoughts about money, and riches, and wealth. Imagine your most prosperous self. Be inspired, and *take action!* I'm rooting for you!

Free Stuff!

Shoot me an email to receive a free gift, the *Money Self-Talk Goodies:* A recorded MP3 file of a Money Self-Talk script.

Email me at:

Kristen@KristenHelmstetter.com

Please specify that you'd like the "*Money Self-Talk Goodies.*"

A Request

I have a favor to ask of you. Would you please write a review for this book on Amazon? Reviews really help me get the word out. Thank you in advance for taking a minute to do so!

Facebook Group

Come join our fun and lively group for readers:

Facebook.com/groups/coffeeselftalk

What's Next?

Here are the other books in the Coffee Self-Talk family:

KRISTEN HELMSTETTER

Wine Self-Talk:
15 Minutes to Relax & Tap Into Your Inner Genius

Looking for more ways to make money? There is an unlimited source of intelligence and creative genius in you. *Wine Self-Talk* is a simple, delicious ritual to help you relax, unwind, and tap into this inner genius. When you do, watch as you start unleashing ideas for growing your wealth. (The wine is optional.)

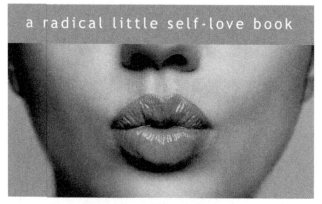

KRISTEN HELMSTETTER

LIPSTICK SELF-TALK

a radical little self-love book

by the bestselling author of
COFFEE SELF-TALK

Lipstick Self-Talk:
A Radical Little Self-Love Book

It's time to make your dreams come true, but you must start with a *rock-solid foundation of self-love.*

Provocative, fun, quirky, and uplifting, *Lipstick Self-Talk* launches you into living your most magical life by teaching you how to *truly love yourself.* Kristen leads you step-by-step with clear insights, sassy words, and poignant stories, showing you how amazing you truly are.

KRISTEN HELMSTETTER

THE COFFEE SELF-TALK™

STARTER PAGES

a quick daily workbook
to jumpstart your
coffee self-talk

a companion to the bestselling book
COFFEE SELF-TALK

The Coffee Self-Talk Starter Pages:
A Quick Daily Workbook to Jumpstart Your Coffee Self-Talk

It has never been easier to dive right into Coffee Self-Talk. This *Starter Pages* workbook takes you by the hand and makes it effortless to get started, with 21 fun, uplifting days of inspiration, affirmations, and simple, fill-in-the-blank exercises to jumpstart your daily Coffee Self-Talk ritual.

The Coffee Self-Talk Daily Reader #1:
Bite-Sized Nuggets of Magic to Add to Your Morning Ritual

This companion book offers short, daily reads for tips and inspiration. It does not replace your daily Coffee Self-Talk routine. Rather, it's meant to be used each day *after* you do your Coffee Self-Talk.

If you do one reading per day, it will take 30 days to complete.

KRISTEN HELMSTETTER

GUIDED JOURNAL

Writing Prompts &
Inspiration for Living
Your Magical Life

The Coffee Self-Talk Guided Journal:
Writing Prompts & Inspiration for Living Your Magical Life

This guided journal keeps you *lit up and glowing* as you go deeper into your magical Coffee Self-Talk journey. Experience the joy of journaling, mixed with fun, thought-provoking exercises, and discover hidden gems about yourself. Get inspired, slash your anxiety, and unleash your amazing, badass self.

5 minutes a day to start living
your magical life

COFFEE SELF-TALK™

KRISTEN HELMSTETTER

International Bestseller – Over 150,000 Copies Sold
Coffee Self-Talk: 5 Minutes a Day to Start Living Your Magical Life

Coffee Self-Talk is a powerful, life-changing routine that takes only 5 minutes a day. What if you could wake up every morning feeling more incredible than ever before... in 5 minutes? **Living the most epic life. Your mind mastered!** Coffee Self-Talk transforms your life by boosting your self-esteem, filling you with happiness, and helping you attract the magical life you dream of living. *All this, with your next cup of coffee.*

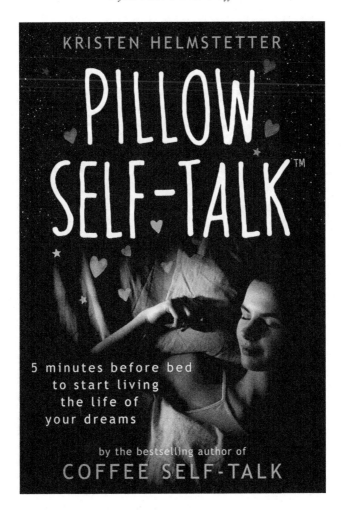

Pillow Self-Talk:
5 Minutes Before Bed to Start Living the Life of Your Dreams

End your day with a powerful nighttime ritual to help you manifest your dreams, reach your goals, find peace, relaxation, and happiness... all while getting the *best sleep ever!*

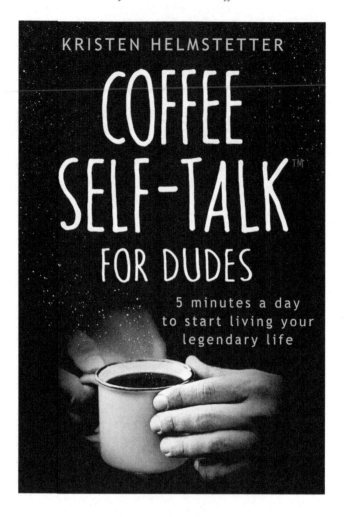

Coffee Self-Talk for Dudes:
5 Minutes a Day to Start Living Your Legendary Life

This is a special edition of *Coffee Self-Talk* that has been edited to be more oriented toward men in the language, examples, and scripts. It is 95% identical to the original *Coffee Self-Talk* book.

Coffee Self-Talk for Teen Girls:
5 Minutes a Day for Confidence, Achievement & Lifelong Happiness

This is written for girls in high school (ages 13 to 17 years old). It covers the same ideas as *Coffee Self-Talk*, and applies them to the issues that teen girls face, such as school, grades, sports, peer pressure, social media, anxiety, beauty/body issues, and dating.

Printed in Great Britain
by Amazon